HBR Guide to
Your Job
Search

Harvard Business Review Guides

Arm yourself with the advice you need to succeed on the job, from the most trusted brand in business. Packed with how-to essentials from leading experts, the HBR Guides provide smart answers to your most pressing work challenges.

The titles include:

HBR Guide for Women at Work

HBR Guide to AI Basics

HBR Guide to Being a Great Boss

HBR Guide to Being More Productive

HBR Guide to Better Business Writing

HBR Guide to Better Mental Health at Work

HBR Guide to Building Your Business Case

HBR Guide to Buying a Small Business

HBR Guide to Changing Your Career

HBR Guide to Coaching Employees

HBR Guide to Collaborative Teams

HBR Guide to Data Analytics Basics for Managers

HBR Guide to Dealing with Conflict

HBR Guide to Delivering Effective Feedback

HBR Guide to Emotional Intelligence

HBR Guide to Finance Basics for Managers

HBR Guide to Getting the Mentoring You Need

HBR Guide to Getting the Right Job

HBR Guide to Getting the Right Work Done

HBR Guide to
Your
Job Search

HARVARD BUSINESS REVIEW PRESS

Boston, Massachusetts

Copyright 2024 Harvard Business School Publishing Corporation

All rights reserved

Printed in the United States of America

10 9 8 7 6 5 4 3 2 1

No part of this publication may be reproduced, stored in or introduced into a retrieval system, or transmitted, in any form, or by any means (electronic, mechanical, photocopying, recording, or otherwise), without the prior permission of the publisher. Requests for permission should be directed to permissions@harvardbusiness.org, or mailed to Permissions, Harvard Business School Publishing, 60 Harvard Way, Boston, Massachusetts 02163.

The web addresses referenced in this book were live and correct at the time of the book's publication but may be subject to change.

Library of Congress Cataloging-in-Publication Data

Names: Harvard Business Review Press, issuing body.
Title: HBR guide to your job search.
Other titles: Guide to your job search | Harvard business review guides.
Description: Boston, Massachusetts : Harvard Business Review
   Press, [2024] | Series: HBR guides | Includes index. |
Identifiers: LCCN 2023033109 (print) | LCCN 2023033110 (ebook) |
   ISBN 9781647825935 (paperback) | ISBN 9781647825942 (epub)
Subjects: LCSH: Job hunting. | Employment interviewing. |
   Job offers. | Job satisfaction.
Classification: LCC HF5382.7 .H425 2024 (print) |
   LCC HF5382.7 (ebook) | DDC 650.14—dc23/eng/20231002
LC record available at https://lccn.loc.gov/2023033109
LC ebook record available at https://lccn.loc.gov/2023033110

ISBN: 978-1-64782-593-5
eISBN: 978-1-64782-594-2

The paper used in this publication meets the requirements of the American National Standard for Permanence of Paper for Publications and Documents in Libraries and Archives Z39.48-1992.

What You'll Learn

Finding a new job can be one of the most daunting parts of your career. No matter how many times you've done it, reading through job postings, updating your résumé, going on interviews, and waiting to hear back can be draining—and time-consuming. The process can feel like a job in itself, and that's on top of your other professional and personal commitments.

But looking for a new role doesn't have to be painful. You can make the process more efficient and manageable, even when you're facing a range of challenging situations: Knowing what kinds of jobs you should apply for, without searching too narrowly or too widely. Turning your skills and experience into a personal brand with a strong narrative. Convincing a hiring manager (or a résumé-scanning tool) that you're the best candidate. Interviewing effectively for a remote job. And staving off doubt and pessimism if the search takes longer than expected.

Whether you're looking for your very first job or the next step in an established career, this guide will help you navigate the ins and outs of landing the role you dream about. You'll learn how to:

- Identify your strengths and what you want in your next job

- Manage difficult emotions throughout your job search

- Conduct informational interviews to explore new opportunities

- Craft a compelling résumé and cover letter

- Answer tricky interview questions—starting with "Tell me about yourself"

- Follow up the right way after an interview

- Figure out if a company's culture is right for you, before you accept an offer

- Negotiate your compensation package, from salary to benefits

- Leave your current job gracefully

- Start a new job well, whether it's remote or in person

Contents

Contents

SECTION TWO

Applying for a Job

SECTION THREE

Acing the Interview

SECTION FOUR

Negotiating Your Offer

Contents

SECTION FIVE

Transitioning into Your New Role

Starting the Search

CHAPTER 1

A Framework for Structuring Your Job Search

by Mimi Aboubaker

Few people find embarking on a job search exciting. In fact, most of us would probably agree that it's a daunting and emotionally exhausting process. As a result, job seekers tend to fall into two broad categories: avoiders and gatherers.

Overwhelmed by feelings of fear or confusion, avoiders often shut down entirely: "I don't know where to start, so I'm going to do nothing." Gatherers, on the other hand, respond to those same emotions with feverish

Adapted from "Finding a Job When You Don't Know What You Want to Do Next," Ascend, on hbr.org, January 28, 2022.

action: "I have no idea what I want to do, so I'm casting a wide net" or "I hate my current job, so I'll apply to everything."

Neither mindset is going to lead you to a successful outcome. In the case of avoiders, idleness does not result in job offers. For gatherers, a lack of clear direction leaves you wandering in many directions.

To land a job you will actually enjoy doing, you need to be intentional about where you apply and why. As part of my own process, I've created what I call a *career and personal manifesto*, a framework to provide structure to any job search. You can use it, too.

Here's how.

The Career and Personal Manifesto

The manifesto has three steps:

1. Evaluate

2. Engage

3. Execute

Evaluate

A successful job search is simple. All you have to do is find job opportunities that match your needs and goals. The hard part is figuring out what those needs and goals are.

To start, spend time with yourself and evaluate your potential next steps. Consider the following six categories, each of which includes a series of questions to help you discover what is the most and the least important to you in your next role.

As you answer these questions, think about your past and present jobs or internships and which aspects of each role you enjoyed the most (or really disliked).

- **Environment:** What kinds of environments, management styles, and ways of working do you thrive in?

- **Role:** What kind of roles and prospects for growth are you looking for?

- **Compensation:** What's the minimum compensation you will accept, and what's your ideal range?

- **Skills acquisition:** What skills and competencies does your résumé currently demonstrate? Are you looking to gain additional skills or further specialize in what you know now?

- **Career narrative:** How does your résumé position you in the hiring market? For example, does it suggest you're someone who cares about socially driven work? Does it suggest you're great at building, launching, and leading new initiatives? Have you collected prestigious company logos?

- **On the horizon:** Is there a meaningful and realistic step you can take within the next 18 months in light of your answers? For example, are there opportunities you can take off the table or add to your list?

Next, use your answers to these questions to fill out a job search prioritization matrix. Doing so will help you figure out which roles to prioritize as you move forward with your search.

Rank the six evaluation categories in order of importance:

1. **Must-haves:** Required—you will not consider any job *without* these items.

2. **Nice-to-haves:** Important—but they won't make or break an opportunity.

3. **No-ways:** Required—you will not consider any job *with* these items.

4. **Don't-cares:** Important—these things don't matter or are nonstarters.

For instance, if compensation is the most important factor to you when you are searching for a new role, then compensation should be the furthest to the left on the matrix. Figure 1-1 is an example of a matrix that has been filled out. This matrix is for a junior consultant who is hypothetically interested in getting a job in the tech industry and who most values skills acquisition and the work environment.

Engage

After working through the questions and filling out the matrix, you should have a better idea of what you are looking to do next. Now, it's time to take action and start

FIGURE 1-1

Job search prioritization matrix

Screening criteria
Organize categories according to level of importance

Most important   ←————————————————→   Least important

Higher ↑

Priority level
Organize attributes according to level of importance
Lower ↓

	Skills acquisition	Environment	On the horizon	Career narrative	Role	Compensation
Must-haves — Nonnegotiables	**New skills:** Build creative problem-solving and critical-thinking capacities **Generalist:** Maintain generalist skill set	**Ways of working:** Dynamic environment; collaborative work streams **Feedback culture:** Continuous, informal feedback	**Entrepreneurship:** Want to build a company and looking to develop new skills critical to running a business	**Experience/skills:** Augment finance background with experience building and scaling a solution and team	**Experience:** Interviewing and hiring for different functions	**Total:** Maintain current compensation
Nice-to-haves — Added bonuses	**Opportunities:** Public speaking **Experience:** Launching new product or new marketing for existing product	**Manager:** Direct; specific in providing instructions and direction **Team:** Disagreement is welcome and encouraged	**Team:** Develop deeper understanding of what it takes to be a highly effective startup employee **Team:** Learn how to coach and manage individuals with different skill sets	N/A	**Projects:** Expansion of service offering into new markets **Industry:** Transportation and logistics (freight, delivery, logistics)	**Equity:** Would be nice to have some ownership in next business
No-ways — Avoid at all costs	**Responsibilities:** Financial modeling and presentation development (developed these skills previously in finance and looking to diversify skill set)	N/A	N/A	**Experience/skills:** Deepening technical skills	**Industry:** Consumer products, consumer applications, personal finance companies	**Total:** Unable to take a step down in compensation because of family planning
Don't-cares — Indifferent about these things	N/A	**Mission:** Not important in next role	N/A	N/A	N/A	N/A

reaching out to people in your network. Discussions are a natural part of the job-hunting process, but you want to segment the people you engage with into two categories:

- **Thought partners:** People who can weigh in on your thinking and path forward (mentors, alumni networks, former managers and colleagues, and so forth)

- **Opportunity sourcers:** People who can help you identify open opportunities

When seeking outside counsel, be wary of what I call advice of convenience, or advice from people who are in your orbit. Advice of convenience is an easy trap to fall into. Instead, try to step out of your comfort zone.

The best people to reach out to for advice are those who (1) you admire, (2) have demonstrated skills and personal attributes you would like to gain, or (3) are doing what you want (or think you want) to be doing. After all, who better to show you the path to where you want to go than the person already there?

Surprisingly, people of all statures are accessible and enjoy offering career advice. There are a variety of channels you can use to reach professionals. The most tried-and-true is LinkedIn, where many professionals have an account. If you use this channel, include a personalized invitation to connect, explaining your objectives to increase the chance of a response.

USING YOUR NETWORK

by Bill Barnett

The best source of potential roles is your network. And the best way to succeed at networking is to reach out broadly. Don't limit your contacts to those you know well—widespread outreach is the only reliable path to success.

Management consultant Isabel provides a good example of active outreach. She targeted three fields and built a list of people to contact by talking to her consulting colleagues and searching alumni databases at her two universities. She also added relevant contacts from search firms. To stay organized, she used a spreadsheet.

Isabel emphasizes how much she learned from simply talking to people—a lot of them: "I had 40 or 50 conversations. Thirty-five were informational. I was talking to anyone who seemed close to being relevant. *What do you do? What do you like?* I was willing to explore any option in my target areas, in some cases if only to learn."

The more she heard, the more she learned. Insights from earlier meetings helped her ask better questions later. She dropped one of her target industries once she realized it didn't match her objectives. People suggested others to contact. Isabel found two good opportunities in three months.

(continued)

USING YOUR NETWORK

Active outreach isn't easy. It requires commitment and organization, but it is absolutely essential. Take these steps:

- *Broadly define your network.* Most people don't realize how many contacts they have. Consider former classmates, colleagues from earlier employers, business relationships outside your institution, and civic acquaintances. People will be flattered that you're asking for help, and they'll likely be happy to assist you.

- *Create a new network along the way.* Ask people whom else to talk to. Consider people you don't know but who are relevant to your search. Cold-call them, email them, ask a mutual contact for an introduction, or reach out on LinkedIn or Instagram.

- *View discussions as learning opportunities, not just job inquiries.* Ask about more than jobs. Ask about the industry, how to succeed, and how to position yourself. Approaching these meetings as conversations breaks the ice. What you learn may lead you to shift your target, as Isabel did, or change the way you present yourself.

- *Be systematic with good record keeping.* Staying on top of broad outreach is complicated. After each meeting, write down what you learned and what you'll do as a result. Use a spreadsheet or another system to track your new knowledge and to gauge progress.

- *Periodically evaluate your progress and whether to change the approach.* View this step as conducting a study. Review your notes from different meetings. Look for patterns. Are there better ways to move in the direction you've selected? Are there different approaches that could help you more? If you see a more effective or efficient way to do something, try it.

Bill Barnett led the Strategy Practice at McKinsey & Company and has taught career strategy to graduate students at Yale and Rice. He is the author of *The Strategic Career: Let Business Principles Guide You.*

Adapted from "Find a Job with Massive, Structured Networking," on hbr.org, December 29, 2011 (product #H0085S).

The basic structure of your message should follow these steps:

- Introduce yourself.

- Establish legitimacy by sharing some background on yourself.

- Clearly explain the purpose of your outreach, including why you want to connect with the recipient (for example, a specific job you have identified at their company, interest in their industry, or interest in learning more about their career path).

- Ask to meet by phone, by video call, or in person.

Sticking with the example of the junior consultant who is interested in transitioning into the tech industry, here is a LinkedIn message they might send to a hiring manager at a company they're interested in:

Hi Ben,

I'm a second-year consultant with casework that includes working with education agencies. I'm looking to transition to edtech startups, and your company piqued my interest.

Would you be open to speaking with me sometime about roles that may match my skill set and interests?

Appreciate any time you can provide, and hope to hear from you soon.

Thanks,
[Your name]

Industries such as technology, media, and fashion also heavily leverage social media platforms such as X/Twitter and Instagram. If the person you are interested in connecting with has a public account, you could send them a public tweet, comment on one of their posts, or send a private direct message, depending on your comfort level. A cold email—similar to the LinkedIn message above—is another option to consider. (Many years ago, I sent an Instagram direct message to the woman leading the U.K. fashion and luxury retail practice of a top technology company, asking to meet while I was in London. We did and we're still in touch!)

Reaching out to people with whom you have affinity will result in higher response rates. They can be high school or college alumni or individuals who like the same sports team or who share your hometown or home state, culture, gender, or professional society.

Once a meeting time has been confirmed, be sure to send a calendar invite with all the appropriate details to the person you are connecting with. You want to make it as easy as possible for them.

Execute

At this stage, work with the contacts you have made in the preceding step to identify a few opportunities that are a good fit for the next stage of your career. Take another look at your evaluation criteria, and determine how your job prospects stack up against each other.

This is where the *opportunities prioritization matrix* comes in. Use it to organize the opportunities you find and prioritize which ones you actually want to apply to. This matrix will save you a great deal of time and energy in your search.

The opportunities prioritization matrix is a loose adaptation of Dwight D. Eisenhower's prioritization framework.[1] Here's how to set it up: Look back at the job search prioritization matrix. Which two categories did you rate as the most important to you? Place these on the two axes (see figure 1-2 for an example) and assess your opportunities to see if they rank high or low (meet or do not meet) those priorities.

The matrix has four quadrants showing three levels of priority:

- **Focus here (one quadrant):** Opportunities in this quadrant are your dream jobs. They meet the two most important criteria you have identified, so you should invest the most time pursuing these.

- **Be mindful of time invested (two quadrants):** These roles match one of your most important criteria but not the other. You will want to use discretion in applying to these positions.

- **Waste of time (one quadrant):** Opportunities in this quadrant rank low for both of your most important criteria. They may not even be worth applying to.

If we use our example of a junior consultant interested in moving into the tech industry, we know that this job seeker has an interest in mission-driven companies and has indicated in a job prioritization matrix that maintaining a generalist skill set and working in a dynamic, collaborative environment are the two most important factors for their next job.

Figure 1-2 shows how the junior consultant might fill out the opportunities prioritization matrix if they were considering certain roles at various companies. You can see that job opportunities that offer generalist skills development (for example, strategy, partnerships and sales, operations) and collaborative team environments land in the "Focus here" quadrant. Job opportunities with a specialized skill set (low match for generalist)

FIGURE 1-2

Opportunities prioritization matrix

Use this tool to help you prioritize which jobs to apply to.

		Skill acquisition	
		High match	Low match
Environment	High match	*Focus here* **Handshake** Special projects **Guild Education** VP, chief of staff **Nova Credit** Enterprise sales	*Be mindful of time invested* **Handshake** Project manager **Guild Education** Product marketing **Nova Credit** Software engineer
	Low match	*Be mindful of time invested* **GitHub** Strategy and operations **Stripe** Corporate strategy **PayPal** Chief of staff	*Waste of time* **GitHub** Product marketing **Stripe** Senior financial analyst **PayPal** Software engineer

and less collaborative environment land in the "Waste of time" quadrant. Since social mission is also important to this candidate, mission-driven companies rank high for fit on environment. Similar positions at non-mission-driven companies rank low on fit when it comes to environment.

All companies and positions have trade-offs, so structuring your matrix in this way allows you to stay laser-focused on the two most important factors as you evaluate opportunities.

For even the most seasoned professionals, the multitude of career paths and job opportunities available can leave you feeling immobilized. By using a structured framework such as this one to focus your efforts, you'll end up with a more favorable outcome and sidestep becoming an avoider or a gatherer.

———————

Mimi Aboubaker is an entrepreneur and a writer. Most recently, she founded Perfect Strangers, the largest U.S. response initiative to the coronavirus crisis. The organization has delivered 3 million meals across the country in partnership with government agencies such as the City and County of San Francisco, the City of Oakland, and the County of Marin. Prior to Perfect Strangers, she founded an edtech venture and spent time at Goldman Sachs and Morgan Stanley. For more tips on leaning in on career and life, follow her on X/Twitter @Mimi_Aboubaker and check out her website at www.mimiaboubaker.com.

NOTE

1. Laura Scroggs, "Avoid the 'Urgency Trap' with Dwight D. Eisenhower's Famous Prioritization Framework," Todoist, https://todoist.com/productivity-methods/eisenhower-matrix.

CHAPTER 2

Job Hunting While Working Full-Time

by Elizabeth Grace Saunders

It's time for a change.

Maybe there's bad management in your workplace, your pay isn't keeping up with your expenses, or you're just feeling burned out. Or maybe you're not feeling any extremely negative emotions toward your current position, but you'd like to do something new, find more opportunities for growth, or simply have greater flexibility and better benefits.

So you tell yourself that it's time to look for a new job. But how? Between maintaining your current position, taking care of home responsibilities, decompressing,

---

Adapted from "Making Time to Job Hunt While Working Full Time," on hbr.org, April 6, 2023 (product #H07KOR).

and getting essentials like food and sleep, you feel as if you just don't have enough time. You don't want to fall behind at work, and your outside commitments fill up a lot of your free time.

As a time management coach, I help many people in this situation figure out how to keep up on their current workload while also carving out time for what's next. I help them plan in an intentional way to get traction and to balance all their responsibilities while still making progress.

Before you even begin a job search, step back and look at your calendar at a high level to decide when to commit yourself to the process. I recommend having at least two or three hours per week to devote to looking for a new opportunity. If you're in a relatively calm time at work and outside the office, this could be the right moment to move forward. But if you are in your busiest period at work, are about to head out on an extended vacation, or are facing a month of playoff games, dance recitals, or other once-a-year commitments, this probably isn't the best season to take on career research. Instead, look for a time when your work should settle down and your home life will be a little less variable. Make a note in your calendar to begin then.

Once you've decided on the right time to get started, follow these tips for fitting a job search into your schedule at four key phases of the process.

Exploration Phase

The first phase of a job search is deciding what you want in a new position. People often desire a new role but don't actually know what they would rather do. If you find yourself in that situation, you'll likely need to do a combination of online research and informational interviews to learn more about opportunities.

In the online research phase, you have an incredible amount of autonomy about when you put in the time. You could pick a regular evening after work, when you know you typically have at least one free hour to explore trends, research the required skills, and take a cursory look at job postings. To make sure that you're consistent, put this commitment into your calendar as a weekly recurring event. And if you struggle to motivate yourself to do the research when you're at home, consider going to a library or coffee shop to give yourself a little extra push (caffeine optional).

For informational interviews, you'll need to accommodate other people's schedules, but you can still be thoughtful about how you fit in the time. If you're serious about finding a new role right now and want to network more, have a designated time each week to think through whom you want to contact and to reach out to them. You could do this step on a weekday evening or morning, or you could carve out some time on the weekends. Put this in your calendar as a recurring event as well.

Once you've heard back from people, schedule the connection time strategically. If the meetings are in person, consider making them early coffee meetups before working hours or happy-hour chats at the end of the day. If the meetings are virtual, you could schedule them almost anytime and consider the call your lunch break. One word of warning, though: If you're looking to watch your timetable, be careful about networking over lunch. Once you factor in driving to an in-person location, you'll be likely to spend more than the typical hour away from your desk. This may be OK if you have the flexibility to make up the time later, but if you're taking long lunches more than once a week, you can easily fall behind.

Preparation Phase

Once you've decided on your general direction, you'll need to prepare to apply. For most people, preparation includes updating their résumés or CVs and sprucing up their LinkedIn profiles (see chapter 6).

In my experience, the preparation phase is often where people get stuck in either procrastination or perfectionism—or both. If you find yourself procrastinating, decide on a specific day and time when you will get started on your updates, such as "this Saturday morning after breakfast." Then devote yourself to that task for an hour or two at the designated time. Once you get to the end of that time block, decide when you will begin again. It's usually impossible to make all the changes you want in a single sitting, but if you consistently move forward, you'll end up making progress.

If you need a little additional encouragement, positive peer pressure could help. That could be from a friend whom you promise to send your LinkedIn profile to for review, a colleague who will proofread your résumé, or a hired coach who will help you navigate through the process. We often feel vulnerable putting ourselves out there, so it can help to surround yourself with supportive people who can give you a nudge, feedback, and encouragement.

If you have refined your résumé and LinkedIn profile but find yourself going back to them again and again to tweak and adjust, you may be falling into the trap of perfectionism. At a certain point, done is better than perfect. If you've had a couple of people look over what you put together and they think it's OK, you're usually better off heading to the next phase of your job search: applications.

Application Phase

The application process will probably look similar to what you experienced in the exploration phase, where you combined online research with informational interviews. Make sure that you're looking within your organization and at companies where you worked previously, because internal hiring and boomerang employees are on trend, as well as at new companies.

You'll probably want to do a quick daily check for new job postings rather than a longer research session once or twice a week as you did in the exploration phrase. Doing these quick checks ensures that you don't miss out on any interesting postings and that you have enough time to complete applications before they're due. Put a recurring daily reminder in your phone or calendar each morning or evening so that you remember to look at any key job posting boards or to at least check your alerts.

If you're in the middle of an application, you might need to devote extended time multiple days in a row to complete it. In these cases, you'll need to do some weekly planning to plot out how this will work with your schedule. Maybe you can start on the application questions this evening but then block out time on the following days in the morning, at lunch, or in the evening to finish it. Look at which time commitments you can move or where you can get help, if needed, to make time to complete the application. For example, maybe you can reschedule lunch with a colleague or ask your partner to do both school drop-off and pickup for the kids for a few days. And you can try to have fewer fixed commitments in your schedule in general when you know that you'll need to be spending a lot of time on applications. Consider pulling back on any big travel plans or volunteer commitments during serious career search time so that you have the flexibility to act when an opportunity arises.

Interview Phase

Depending on the length, timing, and location of your interviews, this phase can be the trickiest part of the process to schedule.

If you work remotely or have a hybrid schedule and the interviews are virtual, schedule them for a day when you're working remotely. If they're short, you can simply count the interview as your lunch break. If they're long, then you'll need to take time off or work early, late, or on the weekend to make up the time. Ideally, you should have the interviews at the beginning of the day, at the end of your day, or around lunch to minimize the disruption to your current work. If you need to interview with multiple people for the same job, you may want to request to do those interviews back-to-back instead of having to schedule them over different days or weeks. If you suggest this option, though, just make sure that you'll be able to keep up your energy over the course of hours of interviews.

If you work in the office full-time or the interviews are in person, you'll very likely need to take time off to cover the time. (Consider saving up your paid time off now!) If possible, ask for the interviews to start right at the beginning of the day or directly after lunch so that you can take a half day off instead of a full day. Also, be careful about booking too many formal meetings for your current job on days when you have an in-person interview. If the interview is running long, you don't want to feel stressed that you're about to miss an important meeting with your boss and seem rushed in the interview. You don't necessarily need to disclose to your manager why you took a half day off, but you *do* need to show up to your 2 p.m. meeting if you said you'd be working that afternoon.

Finding a new job can feel like a job in and of itself. But when you persistently and consistently put time into the process, you can make progress and secure a new position.

Elizabeth Grace Saunders is a time management coach and the founder of Real Life E Time Coaching & Speaking. She is the author of *How to Invest Your Time Like Money* and *Divine Time Management*. Find out more at www.RealLifeE.com.

CHAPTER 3

Get the Most Out of Informational Interviews

by Rebecca Knight

When you're looking for a job or exploring a new career path, it's smart to go out on informational interviews. But what should you say when you're actually in one? Which questions will help you gain the most information? Are there any topics you should avoid? And how should you ask for more help if you need it?

What the Experts Say

"Informational interviews are essential to helping you find out more about the type of industry, company, or

Adapted from "How to Get the Most Out of an Informational Interview," on hbr.org, February 26, 2016 (product #H02P48).

role you're interested in," says Dorie Clark, the author of *Stand Out Networking.* "You may think you already know all about a certain position, but speaking to someone directly gives you the opportunity to test your assumptions." John Lees, a U.K.-based career strategist and the author of *The Success Code*, agrees. Informational interviews "give you exposure—a way to get yourself known in the hidden job market," he says. "The visibility may put you straight onto a short list, even if a job isn't advertised." Whether you're actively trying to change roles or just exploring different professional paths, here are some tips on how to make the most of an informational interview.

Prepare and practice

Informational interviews are, according to Clark, "a safe environment to ask questions." But that doesn't mean you should go in cold. After all, your goal is to come across in a way that inspires others to help you. So do your homework. Study up on industry lingo. Learn who the biggest players are. Be able to talk about the most important trends. You don't want to waste your expert's time asking Google-able questions. "You will come across as a more serious candidate if you are familiar with the jargon and vocabulary," says Clark. Lees concurs. "Showing that you've done your background research plants the idea of credibility in the other person's mind," he says. Work on your listening and conversation skills too. Lees suggests that you practice "asking great questions and conveying memorable energy" with "people who are easy to talk to, such as your family, your friends, and friends of friends."

Keep your introduction short

"What frustrates busy people is when they agree to an informational interview, and then the person seeking advice spends 15 minutes talking about themselves and their job search" instead of learning from them, says Lees. It's not a venue to practice your elevator pitch; it's a place to "absorb information and find stuff out." Clark suggests preparing a "brief, succinct explanation about yourself" that you can recite in three minutes max: "Here's my background, here's what I'm thinking, and I'd like your feedback." People can't help you unless they understand what you're looking for, but this part of the conversation should be brief.

Set the tone

"You want to leave people with a positive impression and enough information to recommend you to others," says Lees. At the beginning of the interview, establish your relationship by revisiting how you were connected in the first place. "Ideally, this person has been warmly introduced to you"—perhaps you have a friend or colleague in common or you share an alma mater—so remind them, he says. It's also a good idea to state at the outset that "you're interested in talking to 10 or 15 industry experts" during your information-gathering phase. "That way, the person will start to process the fact that you are looking for additional sources early on. If you wait until the end to ask for other referrals, she might be caught off guard." Ask about time constraints up front too, says Clark. "If, at the end of the time allotted, you're having a good conversation, say, 'I want to respect your time. I would love to keep talking, but if you need to go, I understand.' Prove you're a person of your word."

Think like a journalist

Prepare a list of informed, intelligent questions ahead of time, says Clark. "You don't necessarily need to stick to the script, but if you're unfocused and you haven't planned, you risk offending the person." Lees recommends approaching your interview as "an investigative journalist would." You're not cross-examining your expert, and you certainly don't want to come across as "pushy or difficult," but you should "gently probe through curiosity, then listen." He suggests a framework of five questions along the lines of Daniel Porot's PIE method (which focuses on pleasure, information, and employment):

- How did you get into this line of work?

- What do you enjoy about it?

- What's not so great about it?

- What's changing in the sector?

- What kinds of people do well in this industry?

You can adapt these questions to your purposes; the idea is to help you "spot the roles and fields that match your skills and experience and give you an understanding of how top performers are described."

Deliberately test your hypotheses

Your mission is to grasp the reality of the industry and the job so that you can begin to decide if they're right for you. So don't shy away from sensitive topics. "You want to hear about the underbelly," says Clark. She suggests questions "designed to elicit the worst information," such as these:

- What are the worst parts of your job?

- What didn't you know before you got into this industry that you wish someone had told you?

Some topics, such as money, may seem taboo but can be broached delicately. Clark gives this advice: "Don't ask, 'How much money do you make?' Instead, say something like, 'I've done some research online, and it seems that the typical salary range is this,' so you're just asking for confirmation of public information."

It's also OK to ask for advice on how to position yourself for a job in the industry by making your experience and skills sound relevant. Clark recommends saying something like, "Based on what you know about my background, what do you see as my weaknesses? And what would I need to do to allay the concerns of a potential hiring manager?" If the feedback is negative, consider it valuable information, but get second and third opinions. "One person's word is not gospel," she says. "You may *not* be qualified, but you also may have spoken to a stick-in-the-mud who discourages everyone. Don't let them limit your career options."

Follow up with gratitude, not demands

While thanking the person for their time via email is a must, Lees recommends also sending a handwritten note to express gratitude right after you meet. "It will help you be remembered," he says. Your thank-you letter needn't be flowery or overly effusive; instead, it should describe how the person was helpful to you and ideally should say that their guidance led to "a concrete outcome" in your job search.

Whatever you do, don't immediately ask for a favor, adds Clark. Not only is it "considered bad manners," but it's also practically "an ambush because you barely know the person." That said, "if, a couple of weeks later, a job opens up at the person's company, you can tell the person you're applying for it and ask if they have any quick thoughts on professional experiences you should play up in your cover letter. If they take the ball and run with it and offer to put in a good word for you, that's great. But do not ask for it."

Play the long game

The real purpose of informational interviews is to build relationships and "develop future allies, supporters, and champions," says Lees. So don't think of them as one-off meetings in which "someone gives you 15 minutes" of their time. Take the long view, and think about ways to cultivate your new professional connection. Forward this person a link to a relevant magazine article, for instance, or invite them to an upcoming conference or networking event. In other words, be helpful. "You want to be seen as giving, not constantly taking," Lees says. Clark notes that it can be a tricky proposition when there's a wide age or professional gap between you, but if you focus on keeping the person "apprised of your progress"—perhaps writing a note saying you read the book this person suggested or that you joined the professional association recommended during the interview—"it shows you listened and that [the] advice mattered."

———————

Rebecca Knight is a future-of-work journalist based in Boston. Her work has been published in the *New York Times,* the BBC, *USA Today,* the *Boston Globe,* Business Insider, and the *Financial Times.* In 2023 she was a finalist for the Reuters Institute Fellowship at Oxford University.

CHAPTER 4

How to Reach Out to a Recruiter

by Marlo Lyons

Recruiters are your best friends when they see you as a potential fit for a job. They also can be as elusive as a yeti when you're trying to get their attention because *you* believe you're the perfect fit for a job.

We usually think of recruiters as people who contact potential candidates, not the other way around. But working with them can be helpful to your job search even if you're the one who reaches out first. Here are three steps to approaching a recruiter in a way that's mutually beneficial.

Adapted from content posted on hbr.org, December 3, 2021 (product #H06Q2G).

Step 1: Know How Recruiters Work

A recruiter's job is to understand each role deeply enough to (1) find the right skills and capabilities for a job they've likely never done themselves and (2) sell you on the position so that you'll accept an offer if you're the best final candidate. Recruiters are part salesperson, part cheerleader, part coach, part therapist, and part strategist to both candidates and hiring managers.

Now picture a recruiter doing all that for multiple job openings at once. Let's say they have five viable candidates per job opening and are managing 10 openings. Yes, most recruiters are managing more than 50 candidates at a time, some of whom may be passive candidates who need convincing to consider new opportunities. If recruiters responded to every random inquiry, they wouldn't have time to fill jobs. That's why it's so critical to reach out to them with a targeted approach.

Step 2: Know What Type of Recruiter You're Targeting

You need to understand exactly which type of recruiter— internal, external, or executive—you're reaching out to and what types of roles they recruit for so that you can position yourself properly.

Internal recruiters

Internal recruiters are assigned to a specific area of their company—for example, engineering, marketing, and finance. So, if you reach out to a finance recruiter for a marketing job, you'll most likely be ignored. Also, a referral from a current employee or someone who knows the recruiter will garner more attention than a generic email. Because internal recruiters tend not to have databases of past candidates, you should keep their name and email in case you find another applicable job at their company.

External recruiters

External recruiters specialize in specific business areas; they don't work for the company with the job opening. For example, some external recruiters recruit only lawyers, while some specialize in industries like entertainment. Many external recruiters don't get paid if they don't find the candidate who ultimately accepts the job. In some instances, they may be competing with an internal recruiter who's also working to fill a role, and if the internal recruiter finds a top candidate, you may lose out if you're the external recruiter's candidate. But don't ignore external recruiters. Many are hired because an internal recruiter has exhausted their search and needs an expert in the field. External recruiters generally do keep databases of candidates because they may be recruiting for similar roles at numerous companies.

Executive recruiters

Executive recruiters can be internal or external and mostly hire at the vice president and higher levels. They do a lot of sourcing for the right candidate and may even seek candidates for confidential roles that aren't posted publicly.

Step 3: Know How to Approach a Recruiter

Reaching out the right way is the most critical step. Never approach recruiters asking them to help you. They don't know you, and you aren't paying them! Their job isn't to help you; your job is to help them do their job and fill roles. Approach a recruiter only after you have done your research, have updated your LinkedIn profile and résumé, are ready to interview, and understand whether the recruiter is internal or external and what types of roles they recruit for.

There are two reasons to approach a recruiter: You may want to be considered for a known position, or you might want to get into the recruiter's database for a desired industry or function.

You can help them fill a current opening

If you can't see the name of the recruiter who posted a particular job, search LinkedIn using the name of the company plus the word "recruiter" or "sourcer" and then read through recruiter profiles to determine their areas of focus. If you can find the one who recruits for the field you're interested in, you'll have a better chance of receiving a response to an inquiry.

Include the job opening you're interested in, and provide the link to the online posting. Describe your applicable skills and capabilities, and describe what value you can bring to the role and company using keywords from the job description. For example:

Hi [Recruiter Name],

I'm reaching out to you directly to express my enthusiasm about the [job opening/link] at [company name]. My extensive experience in [industry or skill] combined with my [hard/soft skills] and unique ability to [unique applicable skill] would make me a tremendous asset to [company name] in this role.

I hope you will seriously consider me for this position and give me an opportunity to explain further how I can bring unique value to the company.

Thank you,
[Your Name]

If you could be right for the role, you may receive a response. If you don't receive a response, it could be a matter of bad timing (the job may be close to being filled), or maybe you're not as right for the role as you think you are.

You're certain the person recruits for a specific industry and function

In this instance, you don't know if the person is recruiting for any specific role, but you do know the types of roles and industries they specialize in. If the recruiter has a role you could fill now, then you may receive a response. Otherwise, they may enter your information into their database for when there's an applicable opening. So, make it easy for them to figure out which roles may be applicable:

Hi [Recruiter Name],

I'm reaching out because I am in the market for a new opportunity, and I understand you recruit for [types of roles]. Here is the type of role where I can bring the most value:

Position: Full-time employee; open to contract work with conversion potential

Title: Director, senior director, or vice president of brand or consumer marketing, B2C

Location: Greater DC area, no farther west than Fairfax County or farther east than Prince George's County; open to relocation to West Coast

Industries: Technology, SaaS, AI, cybersecurity, cryptocurrency, medtech; not interested in ride-sharing or self-driving auto companies

Company: Prefer small startups and companies with fewer than 5,000 employees but open to the right opportunity

Compensation: Negotiable, minimum $100K total comp, including equity; must provide equity

My résumé is attached for your review, and my LinkedIn profile can be found here [link]. I look forward to hearing from you when you have a position where you think I could bring the most value.

Best,
[Your Name]

Finally, keep in mind that all recruiters want to fill job openings quickly and with the right people, but they don't work for you—they work for companies. They are the gateway, not the roadblock, to you securing your next role. If you help them do their job, then not only are you helping make them successful, but you may also land your own dream role.

Marlo Lyons is a certified career, executive, and team coach; an HR executive; and the award-winning author of *Wanted—A New Career: The Definitive Playbook for Transitioning to a New Career or Finding Your Dream Job.*

CHAPTER 5

Managing the Emotional Roller Coaster of a Job Search

by Rebecca Zucker

While a job search can be a time of excitement and hope about new opportunities to come, it can also be a time of great uncertainty and anxiety. Not only will you probably feel the full range of possible emotions during your search, but you may also experience these highs and lows in the span of a single day or week. You might be elated one moment to learn that you are a top candidate

---

Adapted from "How to Manage the Emotional Roller Coaster of a Job Search," on hbr.org, October 18, 2019 (product #H057UF).

for a desired position, only to be disappointed to find out that the job went to someone else. Or perhaps you were unhappy with your performance in a job interview but were later relieved to learn you've still made it to the next round of interviews.

The job search process is fraught with ups and downs, not to mention the angst that comes with the uncertainty about the future of your career and livelihood. Here are a few strategies to manage the emotional roller coaster of the job search.

Know What's Coming

A job search can be as short as several weeks or as long as several months. As with any other process, there are peaks and valleys. One week you have networking meetings and interviews scheduled, people are responding to your emails, and you feel encouraged and hopeful. The next week there is radio silence, making you feel confused, frustrated, or even helpless. Knowing from the start that you will experience these swings in activity and emotion can help prepare you to better anticipate and handle them when they do occur. When you know something is coming, you will be less surprised or shaken by it, as well as less likely to personalize it, and you will therefore rebound and move forward in your search more easily.

Process Your Emotions

Engaging in activities like mindful meditation or journaling can help you process negative emotions as they arise. In contrast to avoiding, suppressing, or ruminating over your emotions—habits shown to be correlated with anxiety and depression—processing your emotions through mindful meditation or journaling involves actually feeling these emotions more fully.[1] It is this ability to experience our emotions, without judging them or trying to change them, that allows us to move through them more quickly and effectively. In a classic study, unemployed engineers journaled about their thoughts and feelings on being unemployed, writing for just 20 minutes a day for five days.[2] Eight months later, 52% had found new jobs, compared with only 18.6% for the combined control groups. In addition, brief mindful meditation creates improved emotional processing and reduced emotional reactivity and has been shown to enhance our emotional processing, even when we're not meditating.

Get Support

Having someone to talk to—such as a career coach, a therapist, or a job search work group—throughout your search can provide much-needed emotional support beyond that of friends and family. An experienced career coach who is an expert in job hunts can also help normalize what you are experiencing and feeling at any given phase of your search and can be a good sounding board for when you are feeling unsure of yourself or what to do next. Like an individual coach, a job search work group can also help you feel a sense of partnership. The group can help mitigate feelings of loneliness that often arise at this time, create a sense of community, and provide tangible help to advance your search.

Engage in Energizing Activities

Make sure your days include activities that energize you, such as exercising listening to your favorite music, or doing some other activity that revitalizes you. Your mood and overall energy level will show in your interactions with others, whether it's a coffee meeting with a former colleague, a networking event, or a job interview. Exercise in particular not only improves mood but also increases self-esteem, sociability, motivation, and cognition and can help you be at your best. David, a client of mine, started exercising daily during his job search. He not only lost 15 pounds and three inches from his waist but also felt mentally and physically stronger, had a greater sense of agency, and was more confident going into interviews.

Put Things into Perspective

It's easy to feel powerless or discouraged when things don't progress in the job search the way we would like. Perhaps a contact hasn't yet made an important introduction for you like they said they would, or a recruiter hasn't gotten back to you in the time frame initially indicated. Although you can send a friendly reminder, take a step back to think about these other people's possible existing priorities. Chances are, your job search isn't in their top five priorities on any given day. This perspective can help you depersonalize the situation and mitigate the negative emotions surrounding it.

Roberta, another client of mine, was deeply depressed when her job search hit the one-year mark after she lost her finance job in the last recession. Her depression, while understandable, created an unproductive cycle of negative thoughts and feelings that kept her paralyzed in her search. I asked her what "Roberta 20 years in the future" would say about her year of unemployment. Without hesitation, she said, "Oh, it's a blip." This "it's a blip" perspective allowed Roberta to emerge from her depressed feelings to not only envision a more successful future but also move forward much more productively. Ultimately, she landed another job as a partner at a top-performing investment management firm.

Feelings are temporary, as are many of the situations that create them (such as a job search). Seeing these challenges as impermanent is a key part of being optimistic, and optimism is associated with higher levels of motivation, achievement, and well-being and lower levels of depressive symptoms.

Using these strategies can help make the inevitable shifts between the highs and lows of the job search more manageable, as well as help you stay motivated and productive for the duration of the ride.

Rebecca Zucker is an executive coach and a founding partner at Next Step Partners, a leadership development firm. Her clients have included Amazon, Clorox, Morrison Foerster, Norwest Venture Partners, the James Irvine Foundation, and high-growth technology companies like DocuSign and Dropbox. You can follow her on X/Twitter @rszucker.

NOTES

1. Simón Guendelman, Sebastián Medeiros, and Hagen Rampes, "Mindfulness and Emotion Regulation: Insights from Neurobiological, Psychological, and Clinical Studies," *Frontiers in Psychology* 8 (March 6, 2017): 220, www.ncbi.nlm.nih.gov/pmc/articles/PMC5337506.

2. Stefanie P. Spera, Eric D. Buhrfeind, and James W. Pennebaker, "Expressive Writing and Coping with Job Loss," *Academy of Management Journal* 37, no. 3 (1994): 722–733, www.jstor.org/stable/256708.

Applying for a Job

CHAPTER 6

Write a Résumé That Stands Out

by Amy Gallo

The résumé: There are so many conflicting recommendations out there. Should you keep it to one page? Do you put a summary on top? Do you include personal interests and volunteer gigs? And how do you make it catch the hiring manager's eye among tons of other ones? A résumé may be your best chance to make a good first impression, so you've got to get it right.

What the Experts Say

"There's nothing quick or easy about crafting an effective résumé," says Jane Heifetz, a résumé expert and the

Adapted from "How to Write a Résumé That Stands Out," on hbr.org, updated December 23, 2020 (product #H01SHP).

founder of Right Résumés. Don't think you're going to sit down and hammer it out in an hour. "You have to think carefully about what to say and how to say it so the hiring manager thinks, 'This person can do what I need done,'" she says. After all, it's more than a résumé. "It's a marketing document," says John Lees, a U.K.-based career strategist and the author of *Knockout CV*. It's not just hiring managers who are your ideal audience. You might also send out a résumé to people in your network who can help make introductions. "In a tough market, your CV has to get you remembered and recommended," he says. (A CV is a complete history of your work and experience, whereas a résumé is a shorter, more focused picture of your background.) Here's how to write a résumé that will be sure to win attention.

Customize it

First things first: Don't send the same résumé to every job. "You can have a foundational résumé that compellingly articulates the most important information," says Heifetz, but you have to alter it for each opportunity. You'll usually need to write the first version in a vacuum, but for each subsequent one, you need context. Heifetz recommends that, as a first step, you carefully read the job description and highlight the five or six most important responsibilities, as well as a few keywords that you can use in your résumé. This exercise should then inform what you write in your summary and which experiences and accomplishments you include. Each version doesn't need to be radically different, but you should "tweak it for the position, the industry, et cetera," says Lees. He suggests that you

Write a Résumé That Stands Out

might change the sequence of the bullet points, for example, or switch up the language in your summary.

Yes, you do need a summary on top

The first 15 to 20 words of your résumé are critically important "because that's how long you usually have a hiring manager's attention," says Lees. Start with a brief summary of your expertise. You'll have the opportunity to expand on your experience further down in your résumé and in your cover letter. For now, keep it short. "It's a very rich, very brief elevator pitch that says who you are, why you're qualified for the job, and why you're the right person to hire," says Heifetz. "You need to make it exquisitely clear in the summary that you have what it takes to get the job done." It should consist of a descriptor or job title like "Information security specialist who . . ." Lees explains, "It doesn't matter if this is the exact job title you've held before or not." It should match what they're looking for. Here are two examples:

- Health care executive with over 25 years of experience leading providers of superior patient care

- Strategy and business development executive with substantial experience designing, leading, and implementing a broad range of corporate growth and realignment initiatives

And be sure to avoid clichés like "highly motivated professional." Using platitudes in your summary or anywhere else in the document is "basically like saying, 'I'm not more valuable than anyone else,'" explains Lees. They are meaningless, obvious, and boring to read.

You may be tempted to skip this part of the résumé, but don't, advises Heifetz. If you're struggling to write it, ask a friend, a former colleague, or a mentor what they would say if they were going to recommend you for a job, suggests Lees. And then use those words. Or you can ask yourself what you'd want someone to say about you if they were making an introduction to the hiring manager.

Get the order right

If you're switching industries, don't launch into job experience that the hiring manager may not think is relevant. Heifetz suggests adding an accomplishments section right after your summary that makes the bridge between your experience and the job requirements. "These are main points you want to get across, the powerful stories you want to tell," she says. "It makes the reader sit up straight and say, 'Holy cow, I want to talk to her. Not because of who she is but because of what she's done.'"

After the accomplishments section, list your employment history and related experience. Then add any relevant education. Some people want to put their education toward the top. Doing so might be appropriate in academia, but for a business résumé, you should highlight your work experience first and save your degrees and certifications for the end.

And that ever-popular skills section? Heifetz recommends skipping it altogether. "If you haven't convinced me that you have those skills by the end of the résumé, I'm not going to believe it now," she explains. If you have expertise with a specific type of software, for example, include it in the experience section. And if it's a drop-dead requirement for the job, also include it in the summary at the very top.

Don't worry too much about gaps

One of the questions that Lees and Heifetz get asked regularly is how to account for gaps in a résumé, perhaps when you weren't working or took time off to care for a family member. If you were doing something that might be relevant to the job during that time, you can include it. Or you might consider explaining the gap in your cover letter, as long as you have a brief, positive explanation. However, the good news is that in today's job market, hiring professionals are much more forgiving of gaps. In a recent survey, 87% of hiring managers said that they no longer see candidates' periods of unemployment as a red flag.

FILLING EMPLOYMENT GAPS ON YOUR RÉSUMÉ

by Vadim Revzin and Sergei Revzin

Lots of job candidates assume that hiring managers favor people who have held several long-term roles. But this is not entirely true. Employers often look for applicants who can illustrate their problem-solving skills and tell stories that prove their capacity to get things done. You can showcase these skills whether or not they are tied to a long-term, nine-to-five job. To potential employers, your abilities are not limited to the tasks you performed in a role. If presented correctly, your skills

(continued)

FILLING EMPLOYMENT GAPS ON YOUR RÉSUMÉ

can be showcased as your experience in a combination of those tasks and as initiatives you have participated in and learned from outside of your primary job.

That said, there's a good chance you're omitting from your résumé some projects or stints that could boost your job search and fill in some gaps. Maybe you took part in a startup competition during school or helped a friend create a social media campaign for their new Etsy store. If you did (or are doing) something interesting in between jobs, something that's helping you develop new skills, include it.

Try this exercise to get you started: Write down every project you've spent time on in between the roles currently listed on your résumé or since you've been unemployed. Now, look at the descriptions of the jobs you're interested in applying to, and see if you can make any connections between your list and what the hiring managers are looking for. Ask yourself, "Have I gained any skills that align with the job requirements?"

Your goal is to reframe your experiences in a way that will help employers draw a connection between the role they are trying to fill and the skills you can offer.

For example, let's say that one of the projects on your list is a podcast that you made during college. You might think that this project has nothing to do with your job search, but if framed right, it could actually add a great deal to your résumé. You could highlight tasks like recruiting guests to the show, preparing them for interviews, and making sure they had a positive time during and after the recording. These experiences show communication and production skills that are valued in a variety of industries.

———————————

Vadim Revzin is a cofounder of School16, an alternative education company that develops skills for nontechnical roles in tech. He is also a professor of entrepreneurship and management at New York University and a cohost of *The Mentors*, a podcast featuring stories from successful founders and creators. He has advised hundreds of entrepreneurs and has been both a founder and a leader across several early- and growth-stage startups.

Sergei Revzin is a cofounder of School16, an education venture that helps professionals acquire skills to break into nontechnical careers in tech, and a cohost of *The Mentors* with his twin brother, Vadim. Previously he was a venture investor at the New York University Innovation Venture Fund, where he led the university's technology investments. Sergei has mentored hundreds of entrepreneurs all over the country through his work with Venture for America and has been an early employee and a founder at tech companies in New York and Boston.

Adapted from "How to Fill an Employment Gap on Your Résumé," Ascend, on hbr.org, February 17, 2021.

Be selective

It's tempting to list every job, accomplishment, volunteer assignment, skill, and degree you've ever had, but don't. "A résumé is a very selective body of content," says Heifetz. "It's not meant to be comprehensive. If it doesn't contribute to convincing the hiring manager to talk to you, then take it out." This advice applies to volunteer work as well. Only include it as part of your experience—right along with your paid jobs—if it's relevant.

So what about the fact that you raise angora rabbits and are an avid Civil War reenactor? "Readers are quite tolerant of non-job-related stuff, but you have to watch your tone," says Lees. If you're applying for a job at a more informal company that emphasizes the importance of work-life balance, you might include a line about your hobbies and interests. For a more formal, buttoned-up place, you'll probably want to take out anything personal.

Share accomplishments, not responsibilities

"My rule of thumb is that 95% of what you talk about should be framed as accomplishments," says Heifetz. "I managed a team of 10" doesn't say much. You need to dig a level deeper. Did everyone on your team earn promotions? Did they exceed their targets? Lees agrees: "Give tangible, concrete examples. If you're able to attach percentages or dollar signs, people will pay even more attention." But you can't and shouldn't quantify everything; you don't want your résumé to read like an accounting report.

Make it readable

Lees says the days of needing a one-page résumé are over: "It used to be that you used a tiny font size, fiddled with the margins, and crammed in the information to make it fit." Nowadays, two or three pages is fine, but that's the limit: "Any more than three, and it shows that you can't edit." Heifetz agrees: "If you're going to tell a compelling story, you'll need more space." You can supplement what's on the page with links to your work, but you have to "motivate the hiring manager to take the extra step required. Don't just include the URL. Tell them in a brief one-line phrase what's so important about the work you're providing," she says.

And stick to the most common fonts and avoid fancy layouts that may not be recognized by online application systems. "It's not how fancy it is [that matters]. It's how clear, clean, and elegant it is in its simplicity," says Heifetz. Vary the line length and avoid crammed text or paragraphs that look identical. The goal is to include enough white space so that a hiring manager wants to keep reading. For example, the opening summary could be three or four lines of text or two or three bullet points. "It just needs to be easy to read," says Heifetz.

Ask for help

It can be hard to be objective about your own experience and accomplishments. Many people overstate—or understate—their achievements or struggle to find the right words. Consider working with a résumé writer, a mentor, or a friend who can help you steer away from questions like "Am I good enough for this position?" and focus on "Am I the right person for the job?" If you do ask a friend for feedback, be specific about what you want them to look out for. Asking a generic question like "Does this look OK to you?" is most likely going to get you a generic response ("Looks fine to me!"). At a minimum, have someone else check for logic, grammar, spelling, and punctuation.

Align your LinkedIn profile

Your LinkedIn profile is just as important as your résumé. You want to make sure you're presenting yourself in the same way. But don't just cut and paste from your résumé. LinkedIn is a different beast altogether, so you want to make the best use of the platform's features. "You don't have to use bullet points; you can be more narrative, and even more casual," says Heifetz. You also want to tweak the tone. "There's a greater expectation that you'll demonstrate personality," she adds. "For example, the summary section should be written in the first person. It gives you the opportunity to present yourself as a living, breathing human being."

Case study: Get an outside perspective

Several months into her previous job, Claire realized that she needed a change. "The job, the industry, and the institution were not the right fit for me. It just wasn't where I wanted to be in my career," she explains. She started to look at job descriptions, homed in on positions or organizations that were interesting to her, and then decided to work with a professional résumé writer. "I tried to do a little changing and reshaping on my own at first, but it didn't feel all that different from where I began," she says. Working with someone else helped her see that the résumé was not about explaining what she'd done in her career but why she was the best person for a particular job.

Claire started with one résumé and then tailored it to each position. "You have the same raw materials—the accomplishments, the skills, the results you achieved over time—but you have to pick and choose to shape those things into a different narrative," Claire says. The summary, which on her résumé consisted of three bullet points, was the element she tweaked the most. For example, when she applied to be an editor, the first bullet point read:

*Versatile **writer** and **editor** committed to speaking directly to readers' needs*

But when she applied for a marketing position, she tweaked it to emphasize her ability to recruit customers and be a brand champion:

*Innovative **brand champion** and **customer recruiter** in marketing, product development, and communications*

Then, before launching into a chronological list of her jobs, she highlighted "selected accomplishments" related to each point in her summary. For example, under "writer and editor," she included three achievements, including this one:

> *Using customer data and email performance metrics, wrote new email series to provide prospective students with more targeted information about Simmons and to convert more of them to applicants. Improved performance over past emails producing average open rates of more than 20%.*

Claire equates collaborating with a résumé professional to working with a personal trainer. She felt challenged to keep rewriting and improving. And the hard work paid off. She recently landed a full-time job.

―――――――

Amy Gallo is a contributing editor at *Harvard Business Review*, a cohost of the *Women at Work* podcast, and the author of two books: *Getting Along* and the *HBR Guide to Dealing with Conflict* (both Harvard Business Review Press, 2022 and 2017, respectively). She writes and speaks about workplace dynamics. Watch her TEDx talk on conflict, and follow her on LinkedIn.

CHAPTER 7

Take These Four Steps Before Applying to a New Job

by Carson Tate

You've revised your résumé. Your LinkedIn profile is up-to-date. The Excel spreadsheet of potential companies, keyword search terms, recruiters, and people to contact in your network is complete.

Let the job search begin—you are more than ready! Right?

Well . . . not so fast.

Adapted from content posted on Ascend, hbr.org, November 23, 2021.

As an executive coach, I see clients fall into this trap all the time. In a fit of excitement or eagerness to begin the application process, they submit themselves to roles without first taking the time to consider what they really want. They think that they can only use their expertise in one way, but this one-track approach drastically limits their potential.

If you want to grow *and* be fulfilled and engaged at work, there are a few things you should consider as you do your search. I recommend a four-step process abbreviated as GROW: *getting* clear on your assets, *recognizing* your results, *owning* your impact, and asking *where and what else*. It's something I've used to help several candidates make smarter decisions about their careers.

Get Clear

If you are not clear on the experiences and capabilities you possess, it's going to be difficult for you to imagine how you can use them to advance in your profession. To land a job you love, you need to be clear on this. Clarity drives success.

To start, let's do a career-plus-life review. This is a powerful process designed to help you methodically assess each professional position you've held in the past. The review should include jobs and internships, volunteer work, and any clubs or hobbies you led or helped organize throughout your education. It's important to reflect on all of these categories because you may have gained experiences and aptitudes that aren't tied to an official J-O-B but that can still be valuable to you now.

The first step involves taking a look at your freshly updated résumé. For your most recent role, write down your answer to the following questions:

1. What is your specific job?

2. What are you responsible for?

3. What do you *do*?

Focus on the *actions* you perform to fulfill your responsibilities—that is, the physical steps you take to get things done. All actions should begin with a verb: *develop, analyze, coach, lead,* and so on. Cross out any abstractions, assumptions, or MBA school jargon. The goal here is to be as clear and as specific as possible.

Now, review your responses to question 3. Identify and highlight the following:

- Themes or clusters of actions that you want to ensure you use in your new job

- Actions that intellectually stimulated, challenged, fulfilled, and motivated you

Consolidate your highlighted items on a separate sheet of paper.

Repeat this process for all your employment and volunteer roles, internships, clubs, and hobbies (even those not listed on your résumé). You will come back to this information later.

Recognize Your Results

To leverage your existing skills, experiences, and talents during the interview process, you need to be able to articulate what they are and the impact you have made with them in the past. Proof of impact is your currency. Your value lies in your ability to show your potential employer that your skills have historically yielded great results. If you're persuasive, you can even use this data to sell yourself for a stretch job, or a role slightly more advanced than what your experience warrants.

Go back to your résumé, and answer the following questions for your current position. Jot down your responses below the actions you highlighted in the previous step. If possible, try to connect your answers back to those actions by thinking about the specific results each of them yielded.

What quantitative outcomes resulted from my actions?

Quantitative results can be counted, measured, and expressed with numbers. Identify each quantitative outcome, and then follow up with a "so what?" question. Numbers without context are meaningless. You need to tell a story about what those numbers mean to communicate the value of the outcome you achieved.

For example, maybe you led an initiative to increase supplier diversity at your organization by 35%. So what? This greater diversity promoted innovation in your company by introducing new products, services, and solutions for your customers. It also provided multiple channels to source goods and services, and it drove competition (on price and service levels) between your company's existing and potential vendors.

What were my qualitative results?

Qualitative results are descriptive and conceptual. They can be based on traits and characteristics.

For example, maybe you managed a group of interns, and because of your leadership skills, one person enhanced their communication skills to be more succinct, precise, and factual. As a result, they were able to quickly resolve customer complaints received on social media and improve the reputation of your brand.

What was my overall impact in the role?

Fill in the blanks:

When I started in this position, our revenue was _____ and our customer service ratings were _____. Over the past year, those numbers have increased by roughly ___% as a result of my efforts doing _____ and _____.

If the preceding metrics aren't relevant to you and your position, replace them with something that is. You might share some data that demonstrates your direct impact on your company, customers, or team. This information doesn't necessarily need to be a hard number—it can be a thank-you note from a client or an example of how you worked with a peer to solve a problem or streamline an outdated process.

For each of your professional roles, answer the preceding three questions to recognize the results you had. You will come back to this data in the next step.

Own Your Impact

In all of your professional positions, you made an impact. Your customers, your team, the company, the community, or an individual was changed because of you and your work. To be fulfilled and engaged in your new job, you must identify the positive feelings associated with the results you uncovered in the prior step.

You may be tempted to skip this step because it appears too soft, woo-woo, or insignificant. I get it. However, there are positive feelings associated with each of your results. These feelings are one of the five elements that help people reach a life of fulfillment and meaning, according to psychologist Martin Seligman, one of the founders of positive psychology.[1]

So, what did you feel when you identified your results? Joy? Hope? Enthusiasm? Pride? Satisfaction?

Go back to the quantitative and qualitative data you identified in the previous step, and note the emotion you felt next to each of your answers.

Where and What Else?

Your final step is to identify where else you can use the actions you identified in the first step (getting clear), particularly those that both created impact (recognize your results) and generated positive emotions (own your impact). This is where all the answers you have written down come together.

For example, let's pretend that in a previous role you were responsible for managing your company's LinkedIn account by creating and posting content, responding to messages, and making connections (your actions). You increased connections by 22% and engagement by 14% (quantitative results). You are proud of your results, and you found joy in the work because it was intellectually stimulating (emotional impact). You know that you want to leverage these skills in your next role.

Now that you've made some connections, it's time to brainstorm how your actions and their impacts demonstrate that you can apply for and get a position beyond the linear journey your résumé may indicate. Think about the following:

- What do you want to do more of in a new position?

- What do your actions show in terms of what you are able to offer an employer?

- How can you use your results to advocate for yourself and take on a more advanced or more engaging role?

- What kind of impact do you need to make to find purpose, joy, or excitement in your work?

Sticking with the preceding example, in which you managed your company's LinkedIn account, perhaps you can leverage this experience to develop content for other marketing channels in your company. Or you might be able to create content for internal company communications. Or maybe you can use this experience to explore a sales position that generates leads through social media.

At the end of the day, you are the architect of your career. Follow the GROW process to be intentional as you conduct your job search and to open doors that were previously unimaginable. The goal is not just a new job. It is a career and work that fulfills, engages, and enables you to reach your full potential.

Carson Tate is the founder and managing partner of Working Simply, a business consulting firm that partners with organizations, business leaders, and employees to enhance workplace productivity, foster employee engagement, and build personal and professional legacies. She is the author of *Own It. Love It. Make It Work.*

NOTE

1. Martin E. P. Seligman, *Flourish: A Visionary New Understanding of Happiness and Well-Being* (New York: Free Press, 2011).

CHAPTER 8

How to Write a Cover Letter

by Amy Gallo

For a lot of people, writing a cover letter is the most challenging (and least enjoyable) part of a job search. There's so much conflicting advice out there, it's hard to know where to start. Here's what to know about crafting a cover letter that will catch the hiring manager's eye.

What the Experts Say

First, you almost always need to write a cover letter when applying for a job. Sure, there will be times when you're submitting an application online and you may not be able to include one, but whenever possible, send one,

---

Adapted from content posted on hbr.org, updated December 23, 2020 (product #H00NTV).

says Jodi Glickman, a communications expert and the author of *Great on the Job*. "It's your best chance of getting the attention of the HR person or hiring manager and an important opportunity to distinguish yourself from everyone else." And in a tight job market, setting yourself apart is critical, says John Lees, a U.K.-based career strategist and the author of *Knockout CV*. Still, as anyone who has ever written a cover letter knows, it's not easy to do well. Here are some tips to help.

Do your research

Before you start writing, find out more about the company and the specific job you want. Of course, you should carefully read the job description, but you should also spend some time looking over the company's website, its executives' X/Twitter feeds, and employee profiles on LinkedIn. This research will help you customize your cover letter, since you shouldn't send a generic one. It will also help you decide on the right tone. "Think about the culture of the organization you're applying to," advises Glickman. "If it's a creative agency, like a design shop, you might take more risks, but if it's a more conservative organization, like a bank, you may hold back."

If at all possible, reach out to the hiring manager or someone else you know at the company before writing your cover letter, advises Lees. You can send an email or a LinkedIn message "asking a smart question about the job." That way, you can start your letter by mentioning the interaction. You might say, "Thanks for the helpful conversation last week" or "I recently spoke to so-and-so at your company." Sometimes, you may be unable to contact the person—or you may not get a response. That's OK. Reaching out to someone in the company is still worth a try.

Focus the letter on the future

While your résumé is meant to be a look back at your experience and where you've been, the cover letter should focus on the future and what you want to do, says Glickman. "It can be helpful to think of it as the bridge between the past and the future that explains what you hope to do next and why." Because of the effects of the Covid-19 pandemic, there may be less of an expectation that you'll be applying for a job that you have deep experience in. "There are millions of people who are making career changes—voluntarily or involuntarily—and need to pivot and rethink how their skill set relates to a different role or industry," says Glickman. You can use your cover letter to explain the shift you're making, perhaps from hospitality to marketing, for example. Think of it as an opportunity to sell your transferable skills.

Open strong

"People typically write themselves into the letter with 'I'm applying for X job that I saw in Y place.' That's a waste," says Lees. Instead, lead with a strong opening sentence. "Start with the punch line," advises Glickman, "why this job is exciting to you and what you bring to the table." For example, you might write, "I'm an environmental fundraising professional with more than 15 years of experience looking to apply my skills in new ways, and I'd love to bring my expertise and enthusiasm to your growing development team." Then you can include a sentence or two about your background and your relevant experience, but don't rehash your résumé.

Chances are the hiring manager or recruiter is reading a stack of these, so you want to catch their attention. But don't try to be funny. "Humor can often fall flat or sound self-regarding," says Lees. Stay away from common platitudes, too. "Say something direct and dynamic, such as 'Let me draw your attention to two reasons why I'd be a great addition to your team.'"

If you have a personal connection with the company or with someone who works there, also mention it in the first sentence or two. And always address your letter to someone directly. "With social media, it's often possible to find the name of a hiring manager," says Glickman.

Emphasize your personal value

Hiring managers are looking for people who can help them solve problems. Drawing on the research you did earlier, show that you know what the company does and some of the challenges it faces. Then talk about how your experience has equipped you to meet those needs. Perhaps explain how you solved a similar problem in the past, or share a relevant accomplishment. You want to provide evidence of the things that set you apart.

Lees points out two skills that are relevant to almost any job: adaptability and the ability to learn quickly. If you have brief examples that demonstrate these skills, include them. Describe what you did and what capabilities you drew on.

Convey enthusiasm

"When you don't get hired, it's usually not because of a lack of skills," says Glickman. "It's because people didn't believe your story, that you wanted the job, or that you knew what you were getting into." Hiring managers are going to go with the candidate who has made it seem like this is their dream job. So make it clear why you want the position. "Enthusiasm conveys personality," Lees says. He suggests writing something like "I'd love to work for your company. Who wouldn't? You're the industry leader, setting standards that others only follow." Don't bother applying if you're not excited about some aspect of the company or role.

Watch the tone

At the same time, don't go overboard with the flattery or say anything you don't mean. Authenticity is crucial. "Even if you've been out of work for months, and would take any job at this point, you want to avoid sounding desperate," says Lees. You don't want your tone to undermine your message, so be professional and mature. A good rule of thumb is to put yourself in the shoes of the hiring manager and to think about "the kind of language that the hiring manager would use with one of the company's customers." It can be hard to discern your own tone in your writing, so you may need to ask someone to review a draft (which is always a good idea anyway—see later advice in this chapter). Lees says that he often cuts out "anything that sounds like desperation" when he's reviewing letters for clients.

Keep it short

Much of the advice out there says to keep it under a page. But both Glickman and Lees say even shorter is better. "Most cover letters I see are too long," says Lees. "It should be brief enough that someone can read it at a glance." You do have to cover a lot of ground—but you should do it succinctly. This is where asking a friend, a former colleague, or a mentor to review your letter can be helpful. Ask them to read it through and point out places where you can cut.

Get feedback

In fact, it's a great idea to share your cover letter with a few people, says Lees. Rather than sending it off and asking, "What do you think?" be specific about the kind of feedback you want. In particular, request two things. First, ask your friend if it's clear what your main point is. What's the story you're telling? Are they able to summarize it? Second, ask them what's wrong with the letter. "Other people are more attuned to desperation, overselling, overmodesty, and underselling" than you are, says Lees, and they should be able to point out places where the tone is off.

When you can't submit a cover letter

Many companies now use online application systems that don't allow for a cover letter. You may be able to figure out how to include one in the same document as your résumé, but that's not always possible, especially because some systems only allow for data to be entered into specific boxes. In these cases, use the format you're given to demonstrate your ability to do the job and your enthusiasm for the role. If possible, you may try to find someone to whom you can send a brief follow-up email highlighting a few key points about your application.

Case study 1: Demonstrate an understanding of what the company needs

Michele Sommers, the vice president of HR for the Boys & Girls Village, a nonprofit in Connecticut, once posted a job for a recruiting and training specialist. "I was looking for someone with a strong recruiting background who could do everything from sourcing candidates to onboarding new hires," she says. She also wanted the person to hit the ground running. "We're a small team, and I can't afford to train someone," she says.

More than 100 candidates applied for the job. The organization's online application system doesn't allow for cover letter attachments, but one of the applicants, Heidi (not her real name), sent a follow-up email after submitting her résumé. "And it's a good thing she did, because she would've been weeded out otherwise," Michele says.

Heidi's résumé made her look like a job hopper—very short stints at each previous employer. Michele assumed she was a poor performer who kept getting fired. Heidi was also the only candidate who didn't have a four-year college degree.

But Heidi's email caught Michele's eye. First, it was professional. Heidi stated clearly that she was writing to double-check that her application had been received. She went on to explain how she had gotten Michele's name and information (through her husband's boss, who was on the board) and her personal connection to Boys & Girls Village (her father-in-law had done some work with the organization).

What really impressed Michele, though, was Heidi's understanding of the group and the challenges it was facing. The applicant had done her research and "listed some things she would do or already had done that would help us address those needs," says Michele.

"The personality and passion she conveyed in the cover letter came through during her phone screening," Michele says. Heidi ended up being more than qualified for the job. "I wanted this role to be bigger from the get-go," Michele recalls, "but I didn't think that was possible. When I met her, I knew we could expand it." Three weeks later, Michele offered Heidi the job and she accepted.

Case study 2: Catch their attention

Over a period of four years, Emily Sernaker applied for multiple positions at the International Rescue Committee (IRC). She never gave up. With each application, she sent a personalized cover letter. "I wanted my cover letter to highlight my qualifications, creative thinking, and genuine respect for the organization," she says.

Sarah Vania, the organization's regional HR director, says that Emily's letters caught her attention, especially because they included several video links that showed the results of Emily's advocacy and fundraising work at other organizations. Emily explains, "I had prior experience advocating for former child soldiers, human trafficking survivors, vulnerable women, and displaced persons. It's one thing to make statements in a cover letter, like, 'I can make a pitch, I am a creative person, I am thoughtful,' but showing these qualities seemed like a better way of convincing the recruiter that the statements were true."

This is what Emily wrote to Sarah about the video:

Here is a short video about my story with activism. The nonprofit organization Invisible Children made it for a youth conference I spoke at this year. It is about four minutes.

As you'll see from the video, I've had a lot of success as a student fundraiser, raising over $200,000 for Invisible Children. I've since gone on to work as a consultant for Wellspring International and have recently concluded my studies as a Rotary International Ambassadorial Scholar.

In each of the cover letters, Emily also made clear how much she wanted to work for IRC. "To convey enthusiasm is a vulnerable thing to do and can come off as naivete, but, when it came down to it, my enthusiasm for the organization was genuine and expressing it felt right," she says. This is how Emily showed her interest:

You should also know that I have a sincere appreciation of the IRC. I have enjoyed learning about your programs and have personally visited your New York headquarters, the San Diego New Roots farm, the We Can Be Heroes exhibit, and the Half the Sky exhibit in Los Angeles. The IRC is my top choice and I believe I would be a valuable addition to your fundraising team.

Throughout the process, Emily learned that the organization had hundreds of applicants for each position and that the positions were extremely competitive. "I appreciated that I wouldn't be the best for every opening but also remained firm that I did have a significant contribution to make," she says. Eventually, Emily's persistence paid off. She was hired as a temporary external relations coordinator, and four months later, she moved into a permanent role.

Amy Gallo is a contributing editor at *Harvard Business Review*, a cohost of the *Women at Work* podcast, and the author of two books: *Getting Along* and the *HBR Guide to Dealing with Conflict* (both Harvard Business Review Press, 2022 and 2017, respectively). She writes and speaks about workplace dynamics. Watch her TEDx talk on conflict, and follow her on LinkedIn.

CHAPTER 9

The Key to Landing Your Next Job? Storytelling

by Janine Kurnoff and Lee Lazarus

Today's workforce is hypercompetitive. It's hard to distinguish yourself, and if you're hunting for a job, you need strategies to appear more credible, authentic, and memorable than your peers.

What's the best approach?

In his bestselling book, *Brain Rules*, molecular biologist John Medina shares a surprising insight that explains why one job candidate's application gets the person noticed while another's lands them in the reject pile: emotion.

Adapted from content posted on Ascend, hbr.org, May 13, 2021.

Recruiters may think they base their decisions purely on logic, but their feelings play just as large a role. It's human nature. Emotions drive how connected we feel to other people, and those connections lead us to perceive someone in either a positive or a negative light. The quickest way to land on the positive side of that equation is simple: Tell a good story on your résumé, in your cover letter, and during your interview.

Storytelling is a powerful tool when it comes to influence and persuasion. Science shows that voicing our opinions is often more polarizing than it is persuasive, and statistics, even when used as evidence, are difficult to retain.[1] But if you blend opinion and statistics and weave them into an engaging narrative, suddenly you can tug at heartstrings and change minds.

All this means you have a lot of power. With the right narrative, you can make anyone you want feel great—about you. All you have to do is organize your ideas into a story that elicits positive emotions, producing a rush of the feel-good hormone dopamine in your listener's brain. As Medina points out, "Dopamine greatly aids memory and information processing. . . . It creates a Post-it note that reads, 'Remember this.'"

Here are four tips that will help you weave storytelling into your next job application—getting you noticed, and ahead, in your career.

Begin with Your Audience in Mind

Increasingly, employers are using artificial intelligence platforms to quickly scan through thousands of résumés and base decisions solely on objective criteria (like keywords that match job descriptions). These are important factors to incorporate into your résumé, which should be tailored to the specific job you're applying for. But the good news is that appealing to a robot recruiter is not incompatible with appealing to a human recruiter behind the screen. You can, and should, try to influence both.

Whether we're fresh out of college or seasoned industry veterans many of us enter the job-hunting process thinking it's best to offer a chronological laundry list of projects and activities we've been part of. Why not? If we jam in as much experience as we can fit into a 45-minute interview or a two-paragraph email, something's gotta click, right?

Actually, the opposite is true.

Let's stop and look at this issue through a business storytelling lens. Is the person receiving this information going to remember *everything*? No way. Would it be wiser to use your time to prioritize the information that will be most relevant to them? Absolutely.

We can't say it enough: Always begin with your audience in mind. What is their role? What is their level? What's going on with their business and industry? What current challenges are most important to them?

Conducting some extra research on LinkedIn, the company website, a corporate report, or through mutual contacts will let you walk in the recruiter's shoes. Then craft a narrative—both through the accomplishments you include on your résumé and through the message you write in your cover letter—of what you bring to the table as a candidate and why you're perfect for the challenges and needs of the company.

And remember, recruiters are looking for more than a list of skills and experiences. They want to hire a candidate who possesses both the technical skills the position requires and soft skills—also known as people skills: authenticity, strong communication, mindfulness, inclusivity, and the ability to bring new perspectives to a team. Resist the temptation to pepper your résumé and cover letters with jargony keywords, and instead be thoughtful about the words you use to convey your voice and tone. You don't want to seem like a cookie-cutter applicant. You want to seem like a real human.

Have a Theme—and Promote It Throughout Your Job Hunt

Now that you know your audience, stop and imagine the *one* thing you want your prospective boss to remember about you above everything else. Before you interact with a recruiter, a hiring manager, or anyone else, be prepared to offer a single simple theme you will leave with them.

In storytelling, this theme is called the *big idea*, and it's the lynchpin of every good narrative. During your job hunt, your big idea should encapsulate precisely what you will bring to an organization and should be woven into all your written and verbal communications.

Are you trying to join a marketing organization? The overarching theme in your application materials could relay "I'm driven by innovation and growth." Every example you cite should point to how you use your creativity to help brands expand their audience. "I grew a marketing department by 50%. I increased clicks on our ads by 30%. Our customer base doubled in two years."

If you are a recent grad just beginning your search, you may be wondering how you can have a theme as someone with a limited employment history. Well, you may not have a lot of job experience, but you do have more than 20 years of life experience, moving through the world with your unique history, mind, and perspective. This experience alone provides you with a great foundation for telling the story of who you are, what you've done, the challenges you've overcome, and the type of employee you'll be if hired.

For instance, let's say you want to join that marketing organization, but you're also fresh out of college. To start, showcase your theme by saying something like "I'm all about boosting brand awareness on social media." From there, cite specific examples from your personal social media accounts, one-off gigs, internships, or school projects. Maybe you can describe how you grew your TikTok following by 50% in a year and how you're excited to help XYZ company do the same. Or maybe you can share how, in your last internship, you helped the marketing team increase the number of newsletter subscribers by 25% in just three months.

Again, all the experiences you cite on your résumé, in your cover letter, and during your interview should directly tie into this single idea. Your theme is not just there to help you take control of your narrative—it is a tool you can use to influence a recruiter's memory of you.

Context! Context! Context!

Throughout the application process, you'll have to tell many stories about yourself and your experiences. Like all great stories, the experiences you talk about will need clear context to resonate with your listeners. Storytelling experts call context the *why* that drives the plot of a narrative. It gives your audience a reason to listen through to the end and arrive happily at your resolution.

Job hunters often make the mistake of leading with their resolution. *I managed a team during my summer job. I built a 50K digital marketing campaign. I implemented a plan to reduce the cost of our supply chain by 25%.* These are all good things to include on your résumé, which will likely be quickly skimmed and used to judge your capabilities.

In your cover letter and during your interview, however, you have a chance to really expand, let your personality shine, and set yourself apart from all the other candidates. You do this through context.

Whether you're just starting out or have years of experience, context is typically established through three things: setting, characters, and conflict. Let's break these elements down:

- **Setting:** The place where the event of your story occurs. Did you launch a product in a past job? Your setting could be the marketplace for this product.

- **Characters:** The people involved in and impacted by the inciting incident of your story. Were you leading a team on campus or managing an important project at work? Were you working with suppliers, volunteers, or interns? Paint the characters in your story to make it (and you) feel more authentic.

- **Conflict:** The inciting incident that causes you and
  the other characters in your story to take action.
  What problem were you trying to solve together? It
  could be a plummet in your sales or even something
  as simple as a disorganized process that needed to
  be optimized. Spelling out the conflict is crucial;
  doing so builds tension and raises the stakes. Think
  of it like this: What makes the hero of a story heroic?
  Saving the day—or resolving some kind of conflict.

As you tell your story, let the context sink in to give
your potential boss or coworker a reason to lean in and
gain a better understanding of how you work with others, approach challenging situations, and solve problems. This is the best way to establish your credibility.

Be the Hero: End Your Story with a Clearly Stated Resolution

With all this context, you've hopefully given your prospective colleague or manager a reason to care about
the outcome of your story. And if you've researched your
audience well, you're highlighting experiences that will
feel relevant to their world.

Now it's time to be the hero and tell them how you
resolved the conflict you had set up. In this part of the
story, you can state those impressive metrics listed on
your résumé but in a lot more detail.

For instance, your résumé might say, "Boosted sales by
15% in the first quarter of the fiscal year." In your cover
letter (and during your interview), you can expand this
resolution into a much more interesting narrative: "One

of my strengths is the ability to pivot strategically under pressure [the big idea]. In my last job, for example, our sales plummeted in mid-2020 because of travel bans brought on by Covid-19 [the conflict]. To work around this, I started thinking about what our customers [the characters] really needed from us during this time and how we could refocus our strategy to serve domestic markets [the setting] with locally produced products. My team [more characters] did this by doing A, B, and C. As a result, not only did we contribute to improving local economies worldwide, but we also boosted our sales by 15% in the first quarter of the next year [the resolution]."

Do you see the difference? One version states a fact, whereas the other breaks down how you solve problems and what you value as an individual: contributing to local communities and bettering the lives of your customers during a challenging time.

You get the idea.

In the end, the resolution you are suggesting is to hire you. Combined, the preceding tools can help you influence any hiring manager to do just that.

Storytelling Is Innate in All of Us

If you're feeling intimidated, remember that you are already a master storyteller. Every time a family member asks you how you are and you respond genuinely, you are telling a story. Every time you recall a funny memory during a conversation with your friends, you are telling a story. Every time you catch up with your coworkers, you are probably also telling some kind of story—about your life, about your mental health, or even about your weekend plans.

Now apply your special skill to your job applications, and see what happens. We promise, it will be good.

Janine Kurnoff is the cofounder and chief innovation officer of the Presentation Company (TPC) and a bestselling coauthor of *Everyday Business Storytelling*. As the visionary behind the company's award-winning storytelling workshops, Janine is passionate about helping talented businesspeople bring clarity and meaning to their ideas and influence decisions through storytelling. For more than 20 years, she has partnered with *Fortune* 500 companies to transform teams into strategic and influential visual communicators.

Lee Lazarus is the cofounder and chief strategy officer of the Presentation Company (TPC) and a bestselling coauthor of *Everyday Business Storytelling*. Together with her sister, Janine Kurnoff, and the rest of their team at TPC, Lee has devoted the past 20 years to helping some of the world's top brands—such as Colgate-Palmolive, Medtronic, and T-Mobile—create captivating, authentic, and influential narratives that drive business forward. Lee believes that no matter their role or function, *anyone* can be a great business storyteller.

NOTE

1. John Baldoni, "Using Stories to Persuade," hbr.org, March 24, 2011, https://hbr.org/2011/03/using-stories-as-a-tool-of-per.

Acing the Interview

CHAPTER 10

Ten Common Job Interview Questions and How to Answer Them

by Vicky Oliver

Interviewing for a new job can be nerve-racking, especially because you don't know what the hiring manager will ask you. Luckily, some questions tend to come up often, which means you can practice and hone your answers ahead of time. Below is a list of 10 common job interview questions, along with answering techniques

---

Adapted from content posted on Ascend, hbr.org, November 11, 2021.

that will help you dazzle your prospects and, hopefully, secure the role you want.

Could you tell me about yourself and describe your background in brief?

Interviewers like to hear stories about candidates. Make sure your story has a great beginning, a riveting middle, and an end that makes the interviewer root for you to win the job.

Talk about a relevant incident that made you keen on the profession you are pursuing, and follow up by discussing your education. In the story, weave together how your academic training and your passion for the subject or industry the company specializes in, combined with your work experience, make you a great fit for the job. If you've managed a complex project or worked on an exciting, offbeat design, mention it.

> *Example:* "I come from a small town where opportunities were limited. Since good schools were a rarity, I started using online learning to stay up-to-date with the best. That's where I learned to code, and then I went on to get my certification as a computer programmer. After I got my first job as a front-end coder, I continued to invest time in mastering both front- and back-end languages, tools, and frameworks."

How did you hear about this position?

Employers want to know whether you are actively seeking out their company, heard of the role from a recruiter, or were recommended to the position by a current employee. In short, they want to know how you got to them.

If someone recommended you for the position, be sure to say their name. Don't assume that the interviewer already knows about the referral. You'll probably also want to follow up with how you know the person who referred you. For example, if you and Steve (who recommended you) worked together previously, or if you met him over coffee at a networking event, mention it to give yourself a little more credibility. If Steve works at the company and suggested that you apply for the job, explain why he thought you'd be the perfect fit.

If you sought out the role yourself, be clear about what caught your eye—bonus points if you can align your values with the company and its mission. You want to convince the hiring manager that you chose this company, over all other companies, for a few specific reasons.

Finally, if you were recruited, explain why you took the bait. Did this role sound like a good fit? Does it align with the direction you want to take your career? Even if you weren't familiar with the organization before being recruited, be enthusiastic about what you've learned and be honest about why you're interested in moving forward with the process.

Example: "I learned about the position through LinkedIn, as I've been following your company's page for a while now. I'm really passionate about the work you're doing in X, Y, and Z areas, so I was excited to apply. The required skills match well with the skills

I have, and it seems like a great opportunity for me to contribute to your mission, as well as a great next move for my career."

What type of work environment do you prefer?

Be sure to do your homework on the organization and its culture before the interview. Your research will save you here. Your preferred environment should closely align with the company's workplace culture (and if it doesn't, it may not be the right fit for you). For example, the company's website may say that it has a flat organizational structure or that it prioritizes collaboration and autonomy. Those are keywords you can mention in your answer to this question.

Maybe the interviewer will tell you something about the company that you didn't uncover in your research, like, "Our culture appears buttoned-up from the outside, but in reality, it's a really laid-back community with little competition among employees." Try to describe an experience you've had that dovetails with that observation. Your goal is to share how your work ethic matches that of the organization.

Example: "That sounds great to me. I like fast-paced work environments because they make me feel like I'm always learning and growing, but I really thrive when I'm collaborating with team members and helping people reach a collective goal as opposed to competing. My last internship was at an organization with a similar culture, and I really enjoyed that balance."

How do you deal with pressure or stressful situations?

The employer wants to know, Do you hold down the fort or crumble under pressure? They want to make sure that you won't have a meltdown when the pressure becomes intense and deadlines are looming. The ability to stay calm under pressure is a highly prized talent.

Share an instance when you remained calm despite the turmoil. If it's a skill you're developing, acknowledge that and include the steps you're taking to respond better to pressure in the future. For example, you could indicate that you've started a mindfulness practice to help you better deal with stress.

Example: "I realize stressful situations are always going to come up, and I definitely have had to learn how to navigate them throughout my career. I think I get better at it with every new experience. While I was working on a new product launch at my last company, for example, things were not going according to plan with my team. Instead of pointing fingers, my first reaction was to take a step back and figure out some strategies around how we could solve the problem at hand. Previously, I may have defaulted to panicking in that situation, so being calm and collected was definitely a step forward and helped me approach the situation with more clarity."

ANSWERING "WHAT IS YOUR GREATEST WEAKNESS?"

by Joel Schwartzberg

Telling a potential employer what you're not good at isn't exactly fun. But resist the urge to put a spin on your answer. Doing so can come across as trite and unoriginal, even scheming. (*My weaknesses? Perfectionism! I work too hard! I care too much!*) The key is to be authentic but not self-sabotaging. An interviewer may remember your answer and hold it against you—even subconsciously—so you need to limit and mitigate any potentially harmful impressions.

These tips can help you respond both responsibly and protectively:

- *Reimagine weakness as a challenge. Even consider replacing the word* weakness *with* challenge *in your answer.* This change in vocabulary removes some of the sting of *weakness* and makes shortcomings seem more fixable, because a weakness implies more permanence than a challenge.

- *Choose skills that are easily correctable through training or commitment.* Work skills like data analysis, presentation skills, or software expertise are typically learnable, and interviewers understand that. But behavior challenges like impatience, disorganization, or insecurity may seem like personality flaws that are harder to overcome.

- *Avoid clichés.* Stay away from overdone examples like "perfectionism" and "being a workaholic" as well as weaknesses that are just strengths in disguise ("Sometimes, I work too hard/research too much/consider too many ideas").

- *Choose a challenge that is not core to the job's responsibilities.* While your strengths should match the skills highlighted in the job description, your challenges should steer clear of those skills. Simply put, you don't want to be weak where the job needs you to be strong.

- *Once you pick a challenge, practice expressing it.* Do so in three parts: the weakness, the minor consequences of the weakness, and your eagerness to address the weakness. Try to incorporate all these elements into your answer, but this time, keep the consequences short, simple, and minor so that you can focus on overcoming the challenge more than on the challenge itself.

(continued)

ANSWERING "WHAT IS YOUR GREATEST WEAKNESS?"

When you put all these tips together, your response should sound like this:

One of my challenges is learning new workplace technologies, like cloud filing platforms, data-base tools, and content management systems. It just takes me longer to learn complicated technology tools. But once I do, I enjoy using them, and I like to help new colleagues learn them as well. I really appreciate it when a com-pany offers classes and resources to help people become confident using the tools.

Joel Schwartzberg oversees executive communica-tions for a major national nonprofit, is a professional presentation coach, and is the author of *Get to the Point!* and *The Language of Leadership*. You can find him on LinkedIn and on X/Twitter @TheJoelTruth.

Adapted from "How to Answer 'What Are Your Strengths and Weaknesses?,'" on hbr.org, May 2, 2023 (product #H07M10).

Do you prefer working independently or on a team?

Your answer should be informed by the research you've done on the company culture and the job in question. Nevertheless, you should expect that most work environ-ments will have some team aspect.

Many positions require you to work collaboratively with other people on a daily basis, while some roles require you to work on your own. When you answer this question, highlight the best traits of your personality and how they fit the job requirements. It could also be in your interest to answer this question by highlighting the advantages and disadvantages of both situations.

> *Example:* "I enjoy a blend of the two. I like having a team to strategize with, get diverse opinions from, and reach out to for feedback. But I am also comfortable taking on assignments that require me to work independently. I find I do some of my best work when I can focus alone in a quiet space, but I really value collaborating with my teammates to come up with the best ideas."

When you're balancing multiple projects, how do you keep yourself organized?

Employers want to understand how you use your time and energy to stay productive and efficient. They're also looking to understand if you have your own system for staying on track with the work, beyond the company's schedules and workflow plans. Be sure to emphasize that you adhere to deadlines and take them seriously.

Discuss a specific instance when you stayed on track. Talk about the importance and urgency of the projects you were working on and how you allocated your time accordingly. Explain how you remain organized and focused on the job in front of you.

Example: "I'm used to juggling projects at my current job, where I'm often moving from one software program to another. I use the timeboxing technique to make sure they're all on track, allocating time on my calendar for certain tasks. I've found that timeboxing really helps me prioritize what needs to get done first, and it holds me accountable for the more repetitive day-to-day tasks I'm responsible for."

What did you do in the last year to improve your knowledge?

Employers want to know how people take initiative to keep learning. You don't have to feel scared about answering this question if you didn't spend your time brushing up on skills or taking courses. We learn from any experience we have.

If you spent time honing your professional skills, you might say the following:

Example: "Lately I've been getting introspective around where I want to take my career. I've read a lot of journals to keep abreast of the latest ideas in my field and sharpened my skills by taking some online courses, such as . . ." (and then be specific).

If you chose to work on your personal development, you could say something like the following:

Example: "A few months ago I decided to spend more time on things I love. So I got back to learning how to play the guitar and journaling. I feel this personal development has brought me closer to myself and has been really great for my mental health and productivity."

What are your salary expectations?

Before you walk into, or log on to, your first interview, you should already know what the salary is for the position you're applying for. Check out websites such as Glassdoor, Fishbowl, or Vault for salary information. You could also ask people in the field by reaching out to your community on LinkedIn.

Employers will always ask this question because every position is budgeted, and they want to ensure that your expectations are consistent with their budget before moving forward.

Remember that it's often better to discuss a salary range rather than a specific number during the interview and to leave room for negotiation. It's also better to err on the side of caution and quote a slightly higher number, as it's easier to negotiate downward than upward. As a general rule, I advise not bringing up questions about salary until your interviewer does or not bringing it up too early in the process.

Example: "In light of my skills, my experience, and the current industry rates, I'm looking at a salary around $X to $Y" (fill in your desired salary range, and give your rationale).

Are you applying for other jobs?

Interviewers want to know if you're genuinely interested in this position or if it's just one of many options you're considering. They simply want to know if you're their top choice. Honesty is the best policy. If you're applying for other jobs, say so. You don't have to necessarily say where you're applying unless you have another offer. But employers might want to know where in the hiring process you are with other companies. You can also mention that you're actively looking for offers if your interviewer asks.

> *Example:* "I've applied to a couple of other firms, but this role is really the one I'm most excited about right now because . . ."

From your résumé, it seems you took a gap year. Would you like to tell us why that was?

Gap years are more popular in some cultures than others. In some professions, gap years may have a negative connotation—the industry moves too fast and you're not up-to-date.

Let your interviewer know that your gap year wasn't about procrastinating over your transition into the working world but that it added value to the confident professional you have become. Depending on what part of the world you're in and how common these breaks are, employers are likely looking to hear stories of what you did and how your experiences have benefited you professionally and prepared you for this role. (For advice on explaining other kinds of gaps in your work history, see chapter 6.)

Briefly explain why you decided to pursue a gap year, and then focus on what came out of it and how that made a positive difference for your future.

Example: "During my last year of high school, I didn't feel ready to choose my educational path, so I took a wilderness course for a few months to sort out my life goals. It may seem a little random, but the time I spent actually helped me develop so many new skills—in the areas of leadership, communication, and [whatever seems appropriate to this position]. During that time, I realized that I wanted to earn a degree in [state your degree] to align with my passion [say what that is]."

To make a winning impression, you'll need to answer each question with poise and passion. But practicing first really helps. Meticulous preparation will allow you to appear confident and in control and will help position you as the ideal candidate when the competition is tough.

———————

Vicky Oliver is a leading career development expert, the author of five bestselling books, including *301 Smart Answers to Tough Interview Questions*, and a nonfiction editor at *LIT*, the journal of the New School master's in fine arts in creative writing program. She's a sought-after speaker and seminar presenter and a popular media source, having made more than 900 appearances in broadcast, print, and online outlets.

CHAPTER 11

Figuring Out If a Company's Culture Is Right for You

by Kristi DePaul

Would you want to work for a company with this job description?

> *We are looking for strong, determined candidates with one to three years of experience. Your boss won't bother to invest in your career development, you won't be able to speak your mind, and your contributions will be of little value to our leadership team. But the salary is great!*

Adapted from "How to Find Out If a Company's Culture Is Right for You," Ascend, on hbr.org, November 30, 2020.

Probably not. Sadly, this description is accurate in more companies than you might think, though they rarely admit it in the real job description. A majority of respondents (61%) to a Glassdoor survey said that they found aspects of a new job different from what they had expected from the interview process. Company culture was cited as one factor that differs most.

Whether you're just starting out or are looking to make a career change, company culture might be the most important thing to consider during your search. In business speak, culture refers to an organization's shared beliefs and values. Culture is often established by leaders and then communicated and reinforced through various methods. It impacts everything from your interactions with colleagues and customers to your advancement, career satisfaction, and mental health.

As a job applicant, you want to find a culture that aligns with your values, that is, the ethics that guide you, fulfill you, and make you feel a sense of purpose. Misalignments on your values—say, an employer insists you work late nights and weekends, or an organization fails to show its commitment to diversity, equity, and inclusion—can affect your day-to-day well-being, dampen your motivation, and, in extreme cases, result in physical illness.

Before the cultural changes spurred by the Covid-19 pandemic, decoding company culture was slightly easier. Just as you can get a sense of a person by walking into their apartment and looking at their books and decor, you can gauge a lot of information by walking into a physical office space. You can get a feel for the people, the layout, and, generally, how things are done.

But now that workplaces are more remote than in the past, how can you actively and deliberately figure out whether an environment is right for you? To gain clarity, I connected with a few experts in this area. Here's what they had to say.

Scour the Internet for Evidence

Almost anything can be found online these days—and that includes a company's culture. You just have to know what to look for.

"Ideally, companies will have a mission, vision, and culture statement accessible online," says Kaleem Clarkson, a cofounder and the chief operating officer of Blend Me. He told me that job seekers should start by paying extra attention to the nuances of language in these messages. Let's look at some ways to tease out company culture online.

Analyze the words used in job descriptions

Pay special attention to how postings are written; their wording can reveal beliefs and priorities that aren't overtly shared. For example, posts that emphasize hustling to meet frequent deadlines and tout perks like happy hours—but give no nod to workplace flexibility—may indicate that work-life balance isn't top of mind. Keep in mind that some keywords may initially sound positive: On the surface, *scrappy* might sound like *resourceful*. But it might actually mean something very different: that a company expects you to do a lot with few resources or that it intends to under-pay you.

Use a gender bias decoder

There are a variety of online tools that read text and analyze its tone for gender bias. Job descriptions that skew more masculine with words like *competitive*, *dominant*, or *leader*, for instance, may result in a lower response from women candidates.

Check out job review boards like Glassdoor

Sometimes even Reddit will have threads about certain organizations, depending on how large or well known the company is. Reading anonymous reviews from current and former employees will give you more insight—with the caveat that not *every* review is accurate. Comments that point to unrealistic workloads or expectations, a lack of growth opportunities, groupthink (especially in more homogeneous industries), or toxic internal cultures are red flags.

Last, do some digging on social media

See what an employer is currently sharing on its channels. Then scroll back to dates around times of controversy or uncertainty to see how it reacted to social movements, civil unrest, instances of racism, or matters of public health. The company's responses in these moments can reveal a great deal about its core values and beliefs.

You might also find that certain organizations demonstrate their most valuable commitments via social media. For example, IBM promotes gender equity through its returnship program—an initiative that helps people restart their careers and that has supported many women who left the workforce to care for family members. Other businesses, like REI, use social media to build awareness around consumerism and its impact on the environment. REI's #OptOutside campaign emerged as an alternative to Black Friday sales, and it embodies the company's ethos.

Uncover What Lies Beneath

Michelle MiJung Kim, CEO of Awaken, recommends taking a more granular approach. "I'm a fan of asking specific questions during interviews," she says. "You can use scenarios to get more detailed answers on the culture. Otherwise, people may default to overly generalized descriptions like 'We're very collaborative!', 'We're results-oriented,' or 'We care about diversity and inclusion.'"

Whether your interview is in person or virtual, Kim advises you to have questions ready ahead of time—and make them as particular as possible. If you ask the right questions, she explains, then you can learn much more than you would expect.

For instance, instead of asking "How would you describe your culture?" try posing more pointed questions, such as these:

- When someone drops the ball on a project, how does your team handle that?

- What specific efforts have been made to create an inclusive culture for underrepresented employees?

- When there is a conflict cross-functionally, how do folks resolve it?

- How does the company ensure a sense of community, even when people are working remotely?

Kim notes that you might still get vague responses. But even that is useful information. Ambiguity indicates that the company hasn't broached the important topics you've raised. Though it's not a positive sign, it's better to know before you accept an offer. You might discover that the company culture doesn't match the package it is trying to sell you. If its good intentions feel transactional rather than genuine, transient rather than impactful, or (even worse) serve only as a PR opportunity rather than a well-grounded policy, then that's a red flag.

Make an Effort to Connect

All of this advice may be helpful if you're still in the interviewing stage, but what if it's too late for that? What if you're reading this chapter and have already accepted the job offer? You can still decode your new company's culture now—even if you're remote.

Lauren Pasquarella Daley, the senior director of the Women and the Future of Work initiative at Catalyst, told me that remote employees should intentionally seek out information by creating opportunities to connect with others once they're hired. (For more on being a new remote employee, see chapter 22.)

"Some organizations will have robust remote onboarding procedures in place, while others may need a few nudges to provide a more inclusive onboarding experience for new employees," she says.

Before your first day, ask these questions:

- Are there any handbooks, sources of online training, or other resources that can help me get a head start and learn more about the company?

- What social platforms is the organization active on?

- Is there a team member who might want to pair up with me as a remote onboarding buddy? (In other words, is there a peer who can teach you about the unwritten rules and norms of the organization?)

"Finally, remember that it is always OK to ask if you need more information or more support," Daley adds. "Building inclusion and equity is important whether someone is in a physical office or working remotely. Small, spontaneous, and frequent social interactions can help create connections in an office—these should still happen when working remotely but may take more intentionality."

No matter what position you find yourself in, use these tips to spot the work cultures that will—and will not—work for you. The company you ultimately choose should enable you to flourish rather than wear you (or your well-being) out.

———————

Kristi DePaul is a Tel Aviv–based entrepreneur and content marketing expert whose writing empowers aspiring professionals to succeed in the ever-changing landscape of work. Her articles have appeared in top international publications, including *HBR's 10 Must-Reads 2024*, and have been cited by leading think tanks and academicians. She serves as CEO of Founders, a globally distributed content agency that supports educational and workforce development organizations around the world. A longtime proponent of working from anywhere, Kristi has been named an international Remote Innovator by Remote and remains an advocate for enhancing others' social and economic mobility through location-independent employment.

CHAPTER 12

Nailing a Remote Interview

by Amy Gallo

Given that many people work from home, there's a good chance that if you're lucky enough to get an interview, you'll be doing it remotely. All of the standard advice about how to prepare for and perform during an interview still applies (see the sidebar for more), but you'll also need to think about other aspects as well.

Technology

When the interview is scheduled, ask what video platform they'll be using and then spend time familiarizing yourself with how it works, especially if you'll need to

---

Adapted from "How to Nail a Job Interview—Remotely," on hbr.org, June 22, 2020 (product #H05OXQ) and "Stand Out in Your Interview," on hbr.org, September 26, 2012 (product #H009G3).

use any features like screen sharing. Test the link ahead of time. Be sure you have a way to reach the interviewer in case the technology fails. "The last thing you want is to be disfluent in a high-pressure situation," advises Art Markman, a professor of psychology at the University of Texas at Austin and the author of *Bring Your Brain to Work*. "People are going to be as forgiving as possible, but if you can demonstrate that you've thought through the contingencies, it'll convey competence." And set up the best possible circumstances for the technology to work. For example, Markman suggests asking others in your household not to stream TV while you're doing the interview.

GETTING THE INTERVIEW BASICS RIGHT

You only get one chance to impress during a job interview. The following steps will help you do just that.

Prepare, Prepare, Prepare

Most people know they need to show up to the interview having done their homework, but Claudio Fernández-Aráoz, a senior adviser at Egon Zehnder International and the author of *Great People Decisions*, says people rarely prepare enough. "You can never invest enough in terms of preparation. You should find out as much as possible about the company, how it's organized, its culture, the relevant industry trends, and some information about the interviewer," says Fernández-Aráoz. He also advises researching the specific job challenges. This knowledge will allow you to demonstrate you have what it takes to fill the role.

Formulate a Strategy

Decide what three or four messages you want to convey to the interviewer. These should "show the connection between what you have achieved and what is really needed to succeed in the specific job and context," says Fernández-Aráoz. Use concise, interesting stories to communicate your messages, and make sure they have a good opening line, such as, "I'm going to tell you about a time that I rescued the organization." Then, learn them like the back of your hand. Whenever possible, use one of your stories to answer an interview question.

Ace the First 30 Seconds

First impressions matter. People who perform best in interviews speak clearly but slowly, walk with confidence, and think through what "props" they will carry so that they don't appear overly cluttered. Try rehearsing how you'll begin the conversation. You can even record yourself on video and play it back without the sound so that you can see precisely how you are presenting yourself and make adjustments.

(continued)

GETTING THE INTERVIEW BASICS RIGHT

Emphasize Your Potential

"No candidate will ever be perfect, and you will be no exception," says Fernández-Aráoz. Instead of harping on where your résumé might fall short—or letting the interviewer do the same—focus on your potential. "If your past achievements are not directly related to the job, but you've demonstrated a great ability to learn and adapt to new situations, you should very clearly articulate that," says Fernández-Aráoz. For example, if you're interviewing for an international role but have no global experience, you might explain how your ability to influence others in a cross-functional role, such as one working between production and sales, proves you can collaborate with different types of people from different cultures.

When It's Going Poorly

There are times when it's clear the interview is not going well. Perhaps the interviewer is not engaged or you stumbled over answers to some important questions. Resist the temptation to agonize over what has already happened. You can also redirect the conversation by acknowledging the situation. You might say something like, "I'm not sure if I'm giving you what you need," and see how the interviewer reacts.

Appearance

Your goal is to look professional. You don't necessarily need to wear a suit jacket, but you don't want to wear a sweatshirt, either. Choose a neutral background for your interview (it probably goes without saying to avoid one of those virtual beach backgrounds). If you have a professional-looking space you can show in the background, it can help humanize you, and it's better than being right up against a wall, according to Claudio Fernández-Aráoz, a senior adviser at Egon Zehnder International and the author of *Great People Decisions*. However, a blank wall can be less risky when it comes to interruptions or accidentally displaying a messy room. You might also consider standing during the interview. "It's more dynamic, your vocal cords warm up faster, and it's easier to project," he says.

Rehearse Ahead of Time

Experiment with how you might answer common questions. "When we get nervous, we tend to start monitoring ourselves," says Markman. "Since you'll be able to see your own image as you're talking during the interview, you're likely to get distracted. Staring at a face—especially your own—will make you lose your train of thought." Be sure to rehearse in the spot where you plan to do the interview so that you can see how you look. If you can't stop looking at yourself when you practice, you might want to close the window with your image in it. You don't want to be self-conscious to the point of distraction. "But it can be useful to occasionally look at yourself during the interview," says Markman, "to make sure you don't have a tag sticking out or something."

Go into the Interview with a Positive Mindset

Remember that during the interview, you won't be getting the same level of nonverbal information from the interviewer. And as Fernández-Aráoz points out, lots of research shows that when we don't have feedback, we tend toward a negativity bias. We think, "This isn't going well." So experiment ahead of time with staying positive and assuming that the best is happening. You might have a mantra you tell yourself when you start to doubt your performance. Or you might sit quietly for five minutes before the interview starts and mentally review all the reasons the interview is likely to go well.

Exaggerate Your Emotions a Bit On-Screen

For the same reason, you want to practice being emotive during the interview. "Unless you have a sophisticated set of earphones, the audio gets compressed and you lose many of the undertones, which convey emotions," Fernández-Aráoz explains. "So you need to exaggerate those a bit." He suggests practicing with a friend on video to "get some feedback about the setting, your tone, and your body language." Your goal is to appear natural and at ease. You might record yourself answering a few sample questions and watch how you appear. But don't do this if you'll just focus on everything you're doing wrong. Again, you don't want to make yourself self-conscious and hinder your performance.

Ask Pertinent Questions

When you are given the chance to ask questions during the interview, Fernández-Aráoz says you should ask all "the usual questions," such as "What are your expectations for this role?" "How will you measure success for the position?" and "What am I not asking you that I should?" Markman suggests also asking about their onboarding process in the virtual environment. How will the company be helping new hires get acclimated?

Looking for a job is never easy, and interviewing for one remotely can be a challenge. By following the advice in this chapter, you can set yourself up to impress the hiring manager and land that dream job—even when you have to do it virtually.

———————

Amy Gallo is a contributing editor at *Harvard Business Review*, the cohost of the *Women at Work* podcast, and the author of two books: *Getting Along* and the *HBR Guide to Dealing with Conflict* (both Harvard Business Review Press, 2022 and 2017, respectively). She writes and speaks about workplace dynamics. Watch her TEDx talk on conflict, and follow her on LinkedIn.

CHAPTER 13

Interviewing Internally? Here's How to Stand Out

by Kelsey Schurer

Applying for a role within your own organization can be more intimidating than applying for the same position at another company. Your team members already know you, or at least they *think* they do.

When we interact with someone regularly, we build up an impression of them in our minds. This is most likely the case with you and your coworkers. They've seen you do one job. They have an idea of what you excel at, your weaknesses, and your quirks. Rewiring the hiring

---

Adapted from "Applying for a Job Internally? Here's How to Stand Out," Ascend, on hbr.org, May 11, 2022.

manager's image of you—whatever it might be—will be difficult. Managers receive around 10 internal applicants for all open positions, and there might also be external candidates vying for the same role. Amid all this competition, you need to help the hiring manager see you in a new light: the best person for the job.

Your mind might jump to the typical job advice, like articulating your skills, relevant experience, or ideas around how the company can grow. Although these tips might help you swim through a strong interview, they aren't going to distinguish you in a sea of applicants, and they aren't going to disrupt how the hiring manager currently sees you. You need to do something bolder. You need to tell the story of who you are—a story the hiring manager won't forget.

The Power of Stories

There are many reasons stories are an incredible mechanism for capturing and holding someone's attention during a job interview. Stories have the powerful ability to transport audiences into a new world. Studies show that they're more likely to stick in a person's memory than facts.

When you share personal stories with people at work, you invite them to see your values, skill set, and purpose through a more intimate lens. This sharing can create a "collision" moment in the eyes of the hiring manager: For the first time, they see your heart and your ambition meet.

Your personal stories also impact how you see yourself. When you present them authentically, you shine a light on your vulnerabilities, extend grace to your faults, and step into a more confident version of yourself by recognizing and owning your truth. This confidence will radiate onto those who know you but who perhaps haven't seen you in that way before.

For these reasons, anyone looking to secure a promotion or a new role within their company can benefit from answering interview questions with personal stories that exemplify why they're great for the job. Here are three tips to help showcase your true self and land that internal role.

Share where you came from before the hiring manager knew you

When a hiring manager doesn't think you're the right fit for a role, they usually feel this way because they know little about who you were before they came to know you. That's why it's important to weave in your background story during the interview. When you're asked an introductory question about why you want the role, don't just focus on what you do currently—talk about where you came from and what your life was like before entering the company.

For example, when I was promoted to hiring manager at my company—a workplace that values storytelling and aims to help writers unleash their stories—I made sure to share with the CEO who I was before the company hired me: someone who had experienced a painful writing community where ostracism, bullying, and subtle manipulation were part of the cohort experience. At the time, I was hungry for a safe place to flourish with other writers and artists. My previous experiences were a huge factor in my decision to join the organization.

That context illuminated why I was a good fit for the managerial role the CEO was looking to fill. Through my story, I showed how and why I valued the company's mission: I wanted to help employ emerging artists and create a safe community in which they could thrive.

In sharing your own background story, make sure to explain why this new role matters to you. Ask yourself, How do my past experiences—in work and life—exemplify the values that this hiring manager might be looking for? Go from there.

Remember, honesty and emotional resonance are essential to vulnerability. Don't be afraid to talk about difficult experiences if they help clarify who you are and why you care about what you do. Having the courage to be vulnerable during an interview displays how you'll model trust with others in the new position.

Be honest about the struggles you've faced in your current role

During the interview, when a hiring manager asks you to talk about your strengths and weaknesses, lean into your road of trials: the challenges you've faced to get where you are today (including the mistakes and embarrassing moments along the way). To err is human. Sharing your obstacles and failures provides context for your growth and shows how you've evolved, grown stronger, or arrived at a more empowered place.

During my own internal interview, I explained that when I began at the company, I experienced growing pains. I was working in areas of storytelling I had never worked in before—business storytelling, marketing, and technical writing. My background was in classical fiction and poetry, and the role was stretching me in new ways. At first, when I couldn't deliver something good enough or fast enough, my work was brushed aside. I failed several times before I succeeded.

It was through practice and the support of my team that I began to grow. My peers highlighted the constraints we all face and helped me find pathways to be poetic and playful in genres I wasn't used to. I learned the importance of creating a psychologically safe work environment. Ultimately, that's what allowed me to take creative risks. I explained to the CEO that I was now more intentional about carving out the space to learn, fail, and try again. I explained that in this new role, that was the kind of team I would want to nurture and cultivate.

By telling a story of your challenges and how you overcame them, you help the hiring manager gain insight into how you've grown and how you will handle similar situations in the future as you take on more responsibility. Among other insights, the manager learns how you might enter difficult conversations, take and implement feedback, and lead others by example in the new job.

Show how you've been courageous at work

When you think of courage, you might think of major heroic acts, like saving someone from a burning building or slaying an evil dragon. When it comes to the workplace, however, courage is simply doing things that scare you. It's being brave enough to ask for help when you need additional support or to apologize for a mistake. It's remaining present, making quick decisions in high-stakes situations, and speaking up when a project falls out of alignment with the company's values. Courage models how you'll fight for the company in the future.

This attribute is deeply important when it comes to leadership and team performance. Studies have shown that companies that build courage and trust have happier, more productive employees. For this reason, it's critical to showcase your acts of courage during the interview. Simply applying for a role internally shows that you're brave enough to embrace change and reach for new opportunities.

When asked what sets you apart from other candidates, show off your courage and your heroic nature. Courage can be noticing what your team members need from you and stepping in to provide it. It can be staying silent and listening. It can be bringing to the surface something that has been gnawing at you. It can be any number of small gestures. The most important thing is telling a story that shows your manager who you are and who you're becoming.

I would be lying if I said I wasn't afraid to tell my CEO about my previous writing community: how I felt ostracized, belittled, and ashamed that I didn't belong, even though I was a writer and an artist just as much as my peers were. Bravery comes in all shapes and sizes. After I shared my story with the CEO, he looked at me and said, "This is exactly why you're meant for this role."

What I thought was a terrible reflection of my identity—a story that showed my rejection, my inability to fit in, my shame of seeming weak in a crowd—he saw as a superpower. In this new role, I could be vulnerable and empathize with other people who were just as hungry to join a safe environment where art can thrive.

Remember that your stories are the gateway to possibility. If you never share who you are, what you're capable of, and why you matter, you'll always wonder, What if?

"What if I'm actually a skilled coach?"

"What if I'm actually a born leader?"

"What if I'm actually an all-star organizer?"

"What if, what if, what if . . .?"

Don't leave these questions unanswered. Take the risk, and use storytelling to illuminate your hero within.

———————

Kelsey Schurer is the director of stories and learning at Round Table Companies, where she specializes in helping leaders, managers, and employees find language to authentically express who they are to the world. She also played an integral role in the creation of the company's Courageous Company Culture program. Previously nominated for a Pushcart Prize, she has received honors include the Virginia Tech Prize presented by the Academy of American Poets, the Louis and Mart P. Hill Award for Outstanding English Honors Thesis, and the regional Scholastic Writing Award presented by the Alliance for Young Artists & Writers.

CHAPTER 14

Get a Great Recommendation from a Job Reference

by Marlo Lyons

Companies usually call your references when you're a finalist for a role. But you may not be the only finalist, and the reference check could determine whether you get the job.

When hiring managers call a reference, they're looking to gain deeper insight into your strengths, development areas, work style, and whether you'd fit into the

Adapted from "How to Get the Best Possible Recommendation from a Job Reference," on hbr.org, August 15, 2022 (product #H076HW).

company culture and team you're trying to join. Here are three steps to ensure that you pick the right references and that they're prepared to discuss why you're the perfect person for the job.

Step 1: Choose the Right References

The most important thing to consider when choosing references is who can be the most enthusiastic about you as a candidate. You might select your former manager who can describe your work in detail, or colleagues from other departments who can speak to your ability to work across a global, matrixed organization. You could even ask external clients who can attest to your ability to influence without authority. Enthusiasm matters as much as what they say about you (if not more).

Hesitation on the part of your reference can ruin your chances of closing the job. When you ask someone to be a reference, ask if they can be an enthusiastic one. If you hear any hesitation, don't list that person. When I was hiring for a role and had two stellar candidates, I called two references for each. The references for one candidate were clearly more enthusiastic and swayed me to hire that person.

Step 2: Prepare Your References

This is your opportunity to prepare your references to focus on the right areas to help you secure the job. At a minimum, you should make sure your references know two things.

First, provide them with the job title and description. Second, they should know what information you want them to convey to the hiring manager. During your interview, did you forget or otherwise omit anything that would be helpful for them to know? For example, maybe you're comfortable working in an ambiguous environment, you're an adaptive learner, or you're good at digging deep to understand a problem before offering solutions.

Be sure to provide examples for whatever information you want your reference to incorporate into their dialogue. If you're not sure what to include, consider the following questions:

- What skill set is critical for the role, and which of your specific skills transfer directly to the role you're applying to?

- Which qualities make you a great candidate for the role? Your ability to align stakeholders? To think strategically and execute? To remain calm under intense deadlines?

- Which qualities make you unique among the other candidates? Would a perspective from your specific background be beneficial to the company?

- Are there any areas of improvement your reference should be able to address? Ensure they have a way to answer a question about your weaknesses or areas for development that you've worked hard to overcome. For example, if you had trouble handing off projects as the company scaled, provide your reference with examples of how you've since overcome that development area and can now quickly adapt to change.

Finally, if you were terminated from a role for performance and gave the recruiter or hiring manager an alternate perspective to explain your departure, make sure your reference is aware of it. Hiring managers and recruiters are searching for one thing that gives them pause. Don't let it be that your reference couldn't answer a question positively with conviction and enthusiasm.

Step 3: Manage Backdoor References

Many employers will seek *backdoor* references, meaning someone who has worked with you but who isn't on your reference list. Those types of references can be more genuine in their characterization of you—or less genuine if they had a direct conflict with you. Unfortunately, the hiring manager may contact such a person, and if you left a company in an unprofessional way and the hiring manager knows someone who works there, it could sink your candidacy. Even if you've grown or learned from the experience since then, your previous behavior may haunt you.

Look on LinkedIn to see if there are mutual connections who may not provide a positive backdoor reference. Perhaps a former colleague is now at the new company where you want to work. If you find mutual connections who know you and your work, determine if it's worth contacting them to discuss their perception of you. Even if you find no connections, recognize that the world is small, and people know people.

When a colleague of mine was in the final stages of interviewing for a new job, the hiring manager asked him delicately if he was still actively working at his current company—the interviewer had heard conflicting information about whether he had departed the company. It was clear the hiring manager knew that my colleague was on a leave of absence, which he had taken to remain employed moments before he would have been fired in a political shake-up. He answered that although he was on payroll, he wasn't working because he was on leave for some short-term medical issues, but he planned to return shortly.

He could hear the skepticism and concern in the hiring manager's voice and knew his candidacy was floundering. He offered to connect the hiring manager to someone who could confirm the leave wasn't more nefarious. The manager called me and dug in deep without asking exactly why the applicant was on a leave of absence. Without revealing my colleague's personal situation or mentioning that, through no fault of his own, he was going to be fired on his return, my enthusiasm and conviction for his work, character, and integrity persuaded the hiring manager to take the final leap and offer him the role. He is now in the C-suite.

The best way to ensure that everyone you work with has something positive to say about you is to build solid working relationships. In every job, find your champions who know your value. If you notice relationships suffering because you may have offended someone or didn't show your best side, consider mending that relationship with a reflection meeting. Discuss your recollection of your work at the time, and explain what you learned or could have done better, even if you believe the other person contributed to the strife. Showing self-awareness and growth may change the perspective of a future backdoor reference. Would you rather be right or employed in your dream job? You can't stop someone from saying something bad about you, but you can grow from every experience and show your growth in the next opportunity.

———————

Marlo Lyons is a certified career, executive, and team coach; an HR executive; and the award-winning author of *Wanted—A New Career: The Definitive Playbook for Transitioning to a New Career or Finding Your Dream Job.*

CHAPTER 15

Four Ways to Follow Up After a Job Interview

by Art Markman

Much of the job application process involves waiting. You check job postings and wait for new opportunities that match your skills and interests. You put together a cover letter and a résumé, send them off, and wait to hear about a possible interview. If you land an interview, you prepare, give it your best shot, and then wait for a response.

The closer you get to an actual offer, the more anxious you are to hear more news. That anxiety creates anticipation and energy. When you are energized, you want to act.

Adapted from content posted on Ascend, hbr.org, November 5, 2020.

But don't. Wait. Once you've had the interview, you need to be smart about how and when you follow up at this stage.

The truth is, there is very little you can do right now that will help your cause. Being overly eager or pushy will (at best) seem annoying and might (at worst) actually hurt your chances of getting the job. Remember that the person who interviewed you may be handling many positions, and if everyone they interviewed reached out to them, their inbox would be inundated with queries.

There are, however, a few exceptions to this waiting rule. More specifically, there are four times when it may be in your best interest to shoot off a note to the hiring manager.

The Thank-You Note

First things first: At the end of your interview, ask the hiring manager when you can expect to hear back from them about the next steps. This date will help you determine when it's most appropriate to follow up down the line.

One day after your interview, you can send your first note. Send a quick email thanking the hiring manager for their time. Keep it short and sweet. Mention one specific thing about the interview or what you learned about their organization. Finally, mention how much you are looking forward to hearing from them. The thank-you note isn't an opportunity to add more content to your interview. It's just a chance to demonstrate your excitement and appreciation. Here's an example:

Dear [Manager's Name],

Thank you so much for your time yesterday and for giving me the chance to share my interest and qualifications for [job]. I particularly enjoyed learning about how your company has a training program for new employees that gives them an overview of different units and career paths.

I look forward to hearing from you.

Best regards,
[Your name]

The Follow-Up Note

If you don't hear back from the hiring manager by the date they mentioned, don't send a note right away. Perhaps you weren't the first choice for the job but you're still in the running. The manager may make an offer to someone else, and that person may not take the job. Give them a little time to work things out.

Put a note on your calendar to follow up one week after that date if you still haven't heard back. When that day comes, send a quick note—no more than three short paragraphs—to the hiring manager you dealt with. The content should be similar to what you wrote for the thank-you note. Express your interest and excitement about the role. Say something positive about the organization, and ask if there is any additional information you can provide that would be of use. Tell them you are looking forward to hearing back soon. Here's how to do it:

Dear [Manager's Name],

I wanted to follow up on my interview on [date] for [position]. I was wondering if you had news to share about the position. I enjoyed our discussion and getting to know more about [company]. Of the companies I have engaged with during my job search, I was particularly impressed by your commitment to training and development. I felt that this growth mindset was a good fit for my career aims.

Please let me know if there is any additional information I can provide. I am excited about the opportunity to work with you at [company].

Best wishes,
[Your name]

The Exception

The one time you can reach out in between the interview and the date the hiring manager gave you is if there is a significant change in your situation or portfolio. If you interview for your dream job and then get an offer from someone else before you hear back, you can write to let them know that you have another offer but that you really admire the company and its mission and are hoping to hear from them before deciding. Or perhaps you have written an article or submitted a patent application relevant to the job you applied for. If the article is accepted for publication or the patent is granted, you can share that news because it might influence the discussions about your application. Here's an example:

Dear [Manager's Name],

I wanted to follow up with you on my interview on [date] for [position]. Since we had a chance to talk, I received a job offer from another firm. However, your role as a leader in the field of [area], along with your commitment to developing the careers of your employees, is impressive, and I am excited about the prospect of working with you. If you have news about the position, I would like to know as I evaluate the offer I am considering.

Best,
[Your name]

The Feedback Note

If you feel like the interview went well, but you aren't offered the job, you can send one additional note to ask for feedback on the interview. Again, you want to be brief. Thank the interviewer again for their time. Say that you enjoyed the interview process and would like to get some constructive feedback on what you can do better in the future to improve your chances of getting a job.

Not all recruiters will take the time to give you that feedback, but you may get a specific tip that can improve your chances next time—and who knows? This improvement could lead to a different job offer down the line. In fact, my oldest son once reached out to get some feedback after being denied an offer, and it turned into a job offer for another position the firm was about to post. Here's what to say:

Dear [Manager's Name],

I was disappointed to learn that I did not get an offer after my interview on [date]. I enjoyed our conversation and am impressed with the work that [company] does. Because I am new to the job search, I was hoping you could give me some feedback on my interview. I would like to ensure that I present myself as effectively as possible in the future. Any suggestions you could give me would be appreciated.

Sincerely,
[Your name]

Finally, remember that job hunting is exhausting. It takes a lot of energy. And it may take longer to get a job than you hoped or expected. It's normal to be restless and tempted to send notes to hiring managers, even if it's just to feel as if you're doing something. Unfortunately, those notes are not going help you get the job. So try your best to channel that energy into something else productive. Volunteer, sign up for networking events, apply to more jobs. Any one of those activities is a good outlet for your energy and is likely to lead to greater opportunities down the line.

Art Markman is the Annabel Irion Worsham Centennial Professor of Psychology, Human Dimensions of Organizations, and Marketing and the vice provost for academic affairs at the University of Texas at Austin. He has written more than 150 scholarly papers on various topics, including reasoning, decision-making, and motivation. His most recent book is *Bring Your Brain to Work* (Harvard Business Review Press, 2019).

Negotiating Your Offer

CHAPTER 16

Fifteen Rules for Negotiating a Job Offer

by Deepak Malhotra

Job offer negotiations are rarely easy. Consider three typical scenarios:

You're in a third-round interview for a job at a company you like, but a firm you admire even more just invited you in. Suddenly the first hiring manager cuts to the chase: "As you know, we're considering many candidates. We like you, and we hope the feeling is mutual. If we make you a competitive offer, will you accept it?"

Reprinted from *Harvard Business Review*, April 2014 (product #R1404K).

You've received an offer for a job you'll enjoy, but the salary is lower than you think you deserve. You ask your potential boss whether she has any flexibility. "We typically don't hire people with your background, and we have a different culture here," she responds. "This job isn't just about the money. Are you saying you won't take it unless we increase the pay?"

You've been working happily at your company for three years, but a recruiter has been calling, insisting that you could earn much more elsewhere. You don't want to quit, but you expect to be compensated fairly, so you'd like to ask for a raise. Unfortunately, budgets are tight, and your boss doesn't react well when people try to leverage outside offers. What do you do?

Each of these situations is difficult in its own way—and emblematic of how complex job negotiations can be. At many companies, compensation increasingly comes in the form of stock, options, and bonuses linked to both personal and group performance. In MBA recruitment, more companies are using "exploding" offers or sliding-scale signing bonuses based on when a candidate accepts the job, complicating attempts to compare offers. With executive mobility on the rise, people vying for similar positions often have vastly different backgrounds, strengths, and salary histories, making it hard for employers to set benchmarks or create standard packages.

In some industries a weak labor market has also left candidates with fewer options and less leverage, and employers better positioned to dictate terms. Those who are unemployed, or whose current job seems shaky, have seen their bargaining power further reduced.

But job market complexity creates opportunities for people who can skillfully negotiate the terms and conditions of employment. After all, negotiation matters most when there is a broad range of possible outcomes.

As a professor who studies and teaches the subject, I frequently advise current and former students on navigating this terrain. For several years I have been offering a presentation on the topic to current students. (To see a video of this talk, go to www.NegotiateYourOffer.com.) Every situation is unique, but some strategies, tactics, and principles can help you address many of the issues people face in negotiating with employers. Here are 15 rules to guide you in these discussions.

Don't Underestimate the Importance of Likability

This sounds basic, but it's crucial: People are going to fight for you only if they like you. Anything you do in a negotiation that makes you less likable reduces the chances that the other side will work to get you a better offer. This is about more than being polite; it's about managing some inevitable tensions in negotiation, such as asking for what you deserve without seeming greedy, pointing out deficiencies in the offer without seeming petty, and being persistent without being a nuisance. Negotiators can typically avoid these pitfalls by evaluating (for example, in practice interviews with friends) how others are likely to perceive their approach.

Help Them Understand Why You Deserve What You're Requesting

It's not enough for them to like you. They also have to believe you're worth the offer you want. Never let your proposal speak for itself—always tell the story that goes with it. Don't just state your desire (a 15% higher salary, say, or permission to work from home one day a week); explain precisely why it's justified (the reasons you deserve more money than others they may have hired, or that your children come home from school early on Fridays). If you have no justification for a demand, it may be unwise to make it. Again, keep in mind the inherent tension between being likable and explaining why you deserve more: Suggesting that you're especially valuable can make you sound arrogant if you haven't thought through how best to communicate the message.

Make It Clear They Can Get You

People won't want to expend political or social capital to get approval for a strong or improved offer if they suspect that at the end of the day, you're still going to say no thanks. Who wants to be the stalking horse for another company? If you intend to negotiate for a better package, make it clear that you're serious about working for this employer. Sometimes you get people to want you by explaining that *everybody* wants you. But the more strongly you play that hand, the more they may think that they're not going to get you anyway, so why bother jumping through hoops? If you're planning to mention all the options you have as leverage, you should balance that by saying why—or under what conditions—you would be happy to forgo those options and accept an offer.

Understand the Person Across the Table

Companies don't negotiate; people do. And before you can influence the person sitting opposite you, you have to understand them. What are their interests and individual concerns? For example, negotiating with a prospective boss is very different from negotiating with an HR representative. You can perhaps afford to pepper the latter with questions regarding details of the offer, but you don't want to annoy someone who may become your manager with seemingly petty demands. On the flip side, HR may be responsible for hiring 10 people and therefore reluctant to break precedent, whereas the boss, who will benefit more directly from you joining the company, may go to bat for you with a special request.

Understand Their Constraints

They may like you. They may think you deserve everything you want. But they still may not give it to you. Why? Because they may have certain ironclad constraints, such as salary caps, that no amount of negotiation can loosen. Your job is to figure out where they're flexible and where they're not. If, for example, you're talking to a large company that's hiring 20 similar people at the same time, it probably can't give you a higher salary than everyone else's. But it may be flexible on start dates, vacation time, and signing bonuses. On the other hand, if you're negotiating with a smaller company that has never hired someone in your role, there may be room to adjust the initial salary offer or job title but not other things. The better you understand the constraints, the more likely it is that you'll be able to propose options that solve both sides' problems.

Be Prepared for Tough Questions

Many job candidates have been hit with difficult questions they were hoping not to face: Do you have any other offers? If we make you an offer tomorrow, will you say yes? Are we your top choice? If you're unprepared, you might say something inelegantly evasive or, worse, untrue. My advice is to never lie in a negotiation. It frequently comes back to harm you, but even if it doesn't, it's unethical. The other risk is that, faced with a tough question, you may try too hard to please and end up losing leverage. The point is this: You need to prepare for questions and issues that would put you on the defensive, make you feel uncomfortable, or expose your weaknesses. Your goal is to answer honestly without looking like an unattractive candidate—and without giving up too much bargaining power. If you have thought in advance about how to answer difficult questions, you probably won't forfeit one of those objectives.

Focus on the Questioner's Intent, Not on the Question

If, despite your preparation, someone comes at you from an angle you didn't expect, remember this simple rule: It's not the question that matters but the questioner's intent. Often the question is challenging, but the questioner's intent is benign. An employer who asks whether you would immediately accept an offer tomorrow may simply be interested in knowing if you are genuinely excited about the job, not trying to box you into a corner. A question about whether you have other offers may be designed not to expose your weak alternatives but simply to learn what type of job search you're conducting and whether this company has a chance of getting you. If you don't like the question, don't assume the worst. Rather, answer in a way that addresses what you think is the intent, or ask for a clarification of the problem the interviewer is trying to solve. If you engage in a genuine conversation about what they're after and show a willingness to help resolve whatever the issue is, both of you will be better off.

Consider the Whole Deal

Sadly, to many people, "negotiating a job offer" and "negotiating a salary" are synonymous. But much of your satisfaction from the job will come from other factors you can negotiate—perhaps even more easily than salary. Don't get fixated on money. Focus on the value of the entire deal: responsibilities, location, travel, flexibility in work hours, opportunities for growth and promotion, perks, support for continued education, and so forth. Think not just about *how* you're willing to be rewarded but also *when*. You may decide to chart a course that pays less handsomely now but will put you in a stronger position later.

Negotiate Multiple Issues Simultaneously, Not Serially

If someone makes you an offer and you're legitimately concerned about parts of it, you're usually better off proposing all your changes at once. Don't say, "The salary is a bit low. Could you do something about it?" and then, once they have worked on it, come back with "Thanks. Now here are two other things I'd like . . ." If you ask for only one thing initially, they may assume that getting it will make you ready to accept the offer (or at least to make a decision). If you keep saying "and one more thing . . . ," they are unlikely to remain in a generous or understanding mood. Furthermore, if you have more than one request, don't simply mention all the things you want—A, B, C, and D; also signal the relative importance of each to you. Otherwise, the negotiator may pick the two things you value least, because they're pretty easy to give you, and feel they have met you halfway. Then you'll have an offer that's not much better and a negotiating partner who thinks the job is done.

Don't Negotiate Just to Negotiate

Resist the temptation to prove that you are a great negotiator. MBA students who have just taken a class on negotiation are plagued by this problem: They go bargaining berserk the first chance they get, which is with a prospective employer. My advice: If something is important to you, absolutely negotiate. But don't haggle over every little thing. Fighting to get just a bit more can rub people the wrong way—and can limit your ability to negotiate with the company later in your career, when it may matter more.

Think Through the Timing of Offers

At the beginning of a job hunt, you often want to get at least one offer in order to feel secure. This is especially true for people finishing a degree program, when everyone is interviewing and some are celebrating early victories. Ironically, getting an early offer can be problematic: Once a company has made an offer, it will expect an answer reasonably soon. If you want to consider multiple jobs, it's useful to have all your offers arrive close together. So don't be afraid to slow down the process with one potential employer, or to speed it up with another, in order to have all your options laid out at one time. This, too, is a balancing act: If you pull back too much—or push too hard—a company may lose interest and hire someone else. But there are subtle ways to solve such problems. For example, if you want to delay an offer, you might ask for a later second- or third-round interview.

Avoid, Ignore, or Downplay Ultimatums of Any Kind

People don't like being told "Do this or else." So avoid giving ultimatums. Sometimes we do so inadvertently— we're just trying to show strength, or we're frustrated, and it comes off the wrong way. Your counterpart may do the same. My personal approach when at the receiving end of an ultimatum is to simply ignore it, because at some point the person who gave it might realize that it could scuttle the deal and will want to take it back. They can do that much more easily without losing face if it's never been discussed. If someone tells you, "We'll never do this," don't dwell on it or make them repeat it. Instead you might say, "I can see how that might be difficult, given where we are today. Perhaps we can talk about X, Y, and Z." Pretend the ultimatum was never given and keep the person from becoming wedded to it. If it's real, they'll make that clear over time.

Remember, They're Not Out to Get You

Tough salary negotiations or long delays in the confirmation of a formal offer can make it seem that potential employers have it in for you. But if you're far enough along in the process, these people like you and want to continue liking you. Unwillingness to move on a particular issue may simply reflect constraints that you don't fully appreciate. A delay in getting an offer letter may just mean that you're not the only concern the hiring manager has in life. Stay in touch, but be patient. And if you can't be patient, don't call up in frustration or anger; better to start by asking for a clarification on timing and whether there's anything you can do to help move things along.

Stay at the Table

Remember: What's not negotiable today may be negotiable tomorrow. Over time, interests and constraints change. When someone says no, what they're saying is "No—given how I see the world today." A month later that same person may be able to do something they couldn't do before, whether it's extending an offer deadline or increasing your salary. Suppose a potential boss denies your request to work from home on Fridays. Maybe that's because they have no flexibility on the issue. But it's also possible that you haven't yet built up the trust required to make them feel comfortable with that arrangement. Six months in, you'll probably be in a better position to persuade them that you'll work conscientiously away from the office. Be willing to continue the conversation and to encourage others to revisit issues that were left unaddressed or unresolved.

Maintain a Sense of Perspective

This is the final and most important point. You can negotiate like a pro and still lose out if the negotiation you're in is the wrong one. Ultimately, your satisfaction hinges less on getting the *negotiation* right and more on getting the *job* right. Experience and research demonstrate that the industry and function in which you choose to work, your career trajectory, and the day-to-day influences on you (such as bosses and coworkers) can be vastly more important to satisfaction than the particulars of an offer. These guidelines should help you negotiate effectively and get the offer you deserve, but they should come into play only after a thoughtful, holistic job hunt designed to ensure that the path you're choosing will lead you where you want to go.

Deepak Malhotra is the Eli Goldston Professor of Business Administration at Harvard Business School and the author of multiple award-winning books, including *Negotiating the Impossible* and *The Peacemaker's Code.*

CHAPTER 17

Strategies for BIPOC to Negotiate Equitable Pay

by Tutti Taygerly

A client of mine recently shared a conversation she overheard at a coffee shop:

> **Person 1:** The recruiter gave me a reasonable offer. I'm happy with it, but I'm going to ask them to double the equity.
>
> **Person 2:** Why double?

Adapted from "5 Strategies for BIPOC to Negotiate Equitable Pay," on hbr.org, April 17, 2023.

Person 1: I don't know. Seems like a good negotiation tactic. Honestly, I'm excited about the offer already.

When you hear this story, what do you think Person 1 looks like?

Most people I've posed this question to picture a white man. If you did too, you're correct. Each one of us absorbs and processes information as we move through the world. When I asked you to imagine Person 1, you most likely associated them with examples you've seen at work or in the media. Research shows that white men are the most likely to ask for a raise among racial groups and genders, and so it makes sense that you'd render that image.[1]

My client, a woman of color, was in the middle of negotiating her own job offer when she overheard this conversation. The salary proposed to her was lower than she would have liked, and the nonchalance of the man's words both amused and inspired her. How could she rise above this lowball offer, especially when she had the obstacle of implicit bias? If you are in a similar situation, the first step is to educate yourself on the racial wage gap.

Understanding the Wage Gap

Despite all the research, advice, and efforts doled out to lessen and close the pay gap, the earning differential for people of color persists. A big factor is the biases marginalized groups face during wage negotiations. Even today, people of color receive lowball offers that put them at a disadvantage and create a huge racial wealth gap.

Over a lifetime, this gap adds up to a loss for Latina, Native, and Black women of about $1 million.[2] While Black or Hispanic job seekers receive lower offers than their white or Asian American peers do, Asian American and Pacific Islander women working full-time are still typically paid just $0.85 for every dollar paid to white men. They lose about $833 every month, and about $400,000 over the span of a 40-year career.

Putting gender aside, Black men also face biases during the negotiation process. They're often perceived as pushy and penalized for bargaining. Altogether, these racial differences ultimately mean that women of color earn 40% lower minimum salaries than white men earn, and men of color earn 30% lower minimum salaries than their white counterparts do.

The Right Way to Negotiate

It's important to acknowledge, first, that the only way to change the status quo is for everyone to openly talk about the problem. The more we call out discriminatory practices, the more pressure we put on organizations and leaders to solve them. Doing this will help empower people of color to self-advocate and negotiate without the fear of consequences. We also have to acknowledge that the problem is systemic; it is not up to workers who are Black, Indigenous, and people of color (BIPOC) to solve the problem.

Even so, if you're a BIPOC currently facing this situation, there are strategies you can use to up your chances of getting the salary you deserve. When faced with an offer that's lower than your expectations, don't shy away from (respectfully) pushing back. Here are five things you can do to successfully negotiate lowball offers.

Do the research

Recruiters will often ask you about your salary expectation at the start of the recruitment process. If you're going directly through the company's website, a hiring manager will typically ask you after the first round of interviews.

Before you answer this question, you need to know three things: the fair market value of the position, broader information about the pay gap for people of color, and the specific context for your role and skills.

Understanding the fair market value of the position can be done though a quick internet search. In the United States, for example, new salary transparency laws are spreading across various states and cities. As of January 2023, California requires employers of at least 15 workers to share the pay range when listing job postings, joining seven other states with pay transparency laws and following initiatives in Norway and Germany. While some countries have made pay transparency legal, other countries consider discussing pay openly an unusual practice. If you find yourself in a situation where the compensation is hidden, know that it's OK to ask the hiring manager or the recruiter what the pay range is once you complete the first round of interviews.

Next, revisit your research around the race and gender pay gaps so that you have the most relevant background data in your pocket. Glassdoor, the Pew Research Center, the World Economic Forum, or country-specific organizations like Statistics South Africa or the Centre for Monitoring Indian Economy are all good sources to find this data. This research is important because it will help you identify whether you end up receiving a fair offer or a lowball one. You need this information to advocate for a proper adjustment.

The third piece of research—understanding how much people make in your role and with your level of skills—is often the most time-consuming. Start having open salary conversations with the people around you, either in your current job or in related jobs across the industry. Having only a little data is actually worse than having no data at all. If you ask your friend from college what they're earning for the same job, for example, you have only one data point, and that could skew your perception. Make sure you speak to a few people to reduce the margin of error on the insights you gain.

While you could try doing this over LinkedIn or in public forums like Fishbowl, it's more likely that you'll get a response by directly reaching out to a trusted colleague or a close peer in another company doing work similar to yours. These conversations can make people feel vulnerable, so be compassionate with yourself and the other person. You can acknowledge the discomfort by saying, "Hey, this is a little awkward, but I'm looking for a new job and hoping to learn as much as I can about fair salaries, especially since people of color historically have a pay gap. I'm happy to share my salary history with you. Would you be willing to do the same?"

After doing this research, you should come away with a salary range in mind, as well as a salary that you know you won't accept. Plan to suggest a higher range rather than a lower range. Negotiating down is often easier than negotiating up.

Know your strengths

Think back to your former jobs or your time in school, and make an exhaustive list of your accomplishments. For example, did you manage funding for an event all by yourself? Were you in charge of the logistics for a new product launch? Did the newsletter you produced smash previous records of open rates and page views? Don't just think about the outcomes. Think about the strengths and skills you had to use to achieve them, and write those down too.

If you find this exercise challenging, ask a trusted coworker or friend to help you. You might say, "I'm taking stock of my strengths as an employee and would love to know if there's anything that's stood out with you while we've worked together." You could also use a third-party assessment like CliftonStrengths (formerly StrengthsFinder).

Finally, consider how your identity as a person of color has helped you in your past workplaces. This information will give you both confidence and negotiation points. For example, maybe your experience with organizing meet-ups for people in your community while also delivering high performance at a full-time job shows that you have entrepreneurial skills that you may use in your next role.

Once you have a list of your accomplishments, review it and narrow down the skills and strengths that are most relevant to the position you're applying for. You should be able to speak to these points throughout the interview process, especially when advocating for the salary you want.

Know what you want

When negotiating, most people focus only on compensation, like base salary, bonuses, a signing bonus, and equity. They forget to spend time thinking through other facets of work that matter to them. Don't make this mistake.

In preparation for the conversation, think about the benefits—beyond money—that are important to you. These could include job title, vacation time, remote workdays, a budget for skills development or educational courses, and tuition reimbursement. Many people of color whom I've coached have negotiated on positional responsibilities and goals. This benefit includes a promise from the employer to meet a future head count, a promise of growth opportunities, a specific budget range for resources, or even the ability to mentor others.

Don't accept the first offer

After sharing your salary range, you will most likely receive an offer. But remember, the initial offer is never the best offer. Most employers expect that you will negotiate and leave room for that.

On receiving the offer, you can inquire, "Is there any flexibility with this number? What's the top and bottom of the range for this role?" Then wait to hear the response.

Most often, there will be flexibility and the employer will follow up by asking what you're looking for. At this point, your research will now come into play. You can say, "Based on my research and my level of experience in X, I'm looking for an offer that's closer to Y."

Overcome implicit bias with directness

As a person of color, if you want to take the negotiation one step further, you can cite race, gender, and the pay gap you've learned about from your research and even your own experience in the workforce. If you've built a connection with the person you're negotiating with, you can be explicit about the systems of implicit bias that BIPOC often face in these scenarios.

Bringing up these inequities will also help you gauge how much the company, or at least the person you're negotiating with, cares about diversity. You should start this conversation with appreciation and focus on the facts—as opposed to pointing a finger at the person (which could result in defensiveness).

For example, you can say, "Thank you for being an advocate of pay transparency; it really shows that your company cares about the pay gap." Then move on to your research. "You may already know that the latest statistics show that a Black woman earns 64 cents to the male dollar."[3] And then, end with the ask: "Given the pay gap, I'm hoping that you might be able to help advocate for some flexibility with my offer."

Finally, as a person of color, you will often be playing the long game. You can take autonomy over the negotiation process by following these steps and making sure to ask for what you want. That's what you're in control of. You have influence over (but not control of) what you get back from the other side. The more you practice negotiating, the better you'll get over time. Every time the racial salary gap is discussed, awareness increases, and that is how change begins.

Tutti Taygerly is an executive coach with 20-plus years of design experience across large companies, design agencies, and startups. She helps cofounders and tech leaders embrace their unique leadership style to achieve professional impact and build a sustainable company culture. She also guides "others" who never felt like they belonged in a professional setting—including women, people of color, and immigrants—to confidently share their voices with the world. Tutti is the author of *Make Space to Lead* and the forthcoming *Hardworking Rebels: How Asian American Women Claim Their Integrated Leadership*.

NOTES

1. Kerry Jones, "Gender Can Be a Bigger Factor Than Race in Raise Negotiations," hbr.org, September 1, 2016, https://hbr.org/2016/09/gender-can-be-a-bigger-factor-than-race-in-raise-negotiations.

2. Jasmine Tucker, "The Wage Gap Robs Women Working Full Time, Year Round of Hundreds of Thousands of Dollars Over a Lifetime," fact sheet, National Women's Law Center, March 2023, https://nwlc.org/resource/the-wage-gap-robs-women-working-full-time-year-round-of-hundreds-of-thousands-of-dollars-over-a-lifetime/#.

3. Robin Bleiweis, Jocelyn Frye, and Rose Khattar, "Women of Color and the Wage Gap," Center for American Progress, November 17, 2021, www.americanprogress.org/article/women-of-color-and-the-wage-gap.

CHAPTER 18

Managing a Job Offer When You're Still Interviewing Elsewhere

by Marlo Lyons

After months of interviewing for new jobs, you finally have an offer in hand. You're excited, but it's not your first choice. You're still interviewing for your dream job and some other ones you don't know enough about yet. You don't want to lose the current offer, but at the same time, you want to see how the other companies' hiring

---

Adapted from "How to Manage a Job Offer When You're Still Interviewing Elsewhere," on hbr.org, March 23, 2022 (product #H06WJU).

processes play out. What should you do? Here are five ways to manage an offer in hand when you don't know if or when another will come.

Ask for Time to Decide

The most important thing to do is express excitement. Without setting a positive tone, you risk having the offer pulled back. By letting a recruiter know you're excited about the job and company and grateful to have the offer, you're showing that you're invested in potentially joining their company.

Then you can ask for up to one week to consider the offer. Gauge the recruiter's reaction. Some companies won't want to wait that long, because the market is so competitive, and the company will want to know if it needs to move to a backup candidate or start the search all over again. If the recruiter's reaction is chilly, ask them what a reasonable time is to give a response—without providing more detail. You don't want to tell them you're still interviewing, because it will leave the impression that your excitement about the role isn't authentic.

Meet More People or Take a Tour

If you can't control how much time you have to consider the offer, you can try to extend the timeline by asking to meet with someone you haven't met with yet or to take a tour of the office (if applicable) before making a decision. Taking a tour, even of an empty office, will help you get a sense of the culture and collaborative spaces. Try to schedule the meeting or tour a week out, which will give you a chance to finish interviewing with other companies.

Reject Companies You're Not Interested In

During that period, if you've been interviewing at companies you're not as interested in, call or email the recruiters to inform them that you have an offer and plan to accept. While most candidates have been ghosted by a recruiter at some point in their job search, don't mimic poor behavior. You've built a relationship with them, and you may need it in a few years. Treat recruiters with the respect you'd hope to be treated with, even if you've had previous bad experiences.

Determine If You're a Viable Candidate Elsewhere

Contact the recruiter or the hiring manager from your first-choice company to reiterate your excitement for their job, and let them that know that they're your first choice but that you have an offer from your second-choice company. Mention that you wouldn't want to lose the offer if you're not a viable candidate for the first-choice job, ask if you're truly in the running, and listen carefully to the energy in the response. If they say you aren't a viable candidate, you can move on. If they say they're just starting the recruitment process, that means that as great as you may be, they're willing to lose you as a candidate.

If they say you are a viable candidate, there's great enthusiasm, and you're far along in the interview process, you can ask if there's anything else you can answer for them to make an offer. If it's early in the interview process, you can ask them to expedite the rest of the process to determine whether you're the best candidate for the job. If they can speed things up, great! If they can't, then you'll need to decide whether you want to take the risk of rejecting the offer you already have.

Take the Job and Ask for a Delayed Start

The average new hire will start a new job between two and four weeks after accepting an offer. If you can sustain it financially, ask for a start date a month out. This delay will give you time to finish the interview process with any other companies to determine whether they're a better fit. There are pros and cons to taking this approach.

Pros

If you accept, you'll have a job waiting for you, so you won't feel as much pressure to land another offer. Asking for four weeks will also give you time to either successfully receive an offer from your first-choice company or exhaust your other options. These actions will allow you to become fully invested in the job you accepted.

Cons

If you wait a month and you're currently unemployed, you could be without a paycheck for that period, which could lead to financial hardship. Even if finances are not a concern, changing your mind after accepting an offer could reflect poorly on your character, especially if you don't handle uncomfortable conversations well.

If you want to accept an offer from another company after you've already accepted one elsewhere, it's best to call the recruiter from the company you planned to join as soon as possible and inform them that you changed your mind. You may think an email is fine, but a phone call with an apology is better, no matter how uncomfortable it may be. I remember a new hire not showing up to his first day of work, and calls and texts going unanswered. Knowing he was driving a long distance for his first day, the recruiter sent police to his home to check that everything was all right—and the new employee opened the door. Afterward, he sent a nasty email to the recruiter, saying the person had "gone too far sending police to my home." He had just changed his mind and didn't find it necessary to tell anyone.

It will take the rejected company another 60-plus days to make a new hire, so don't ghost the company or delay informing them. Even if you handle this conversation perfectly, you may never work at the rejected company again or at other companies where the recruiter and hiring manager move on to later.

In the end, you want to find the right fit for you, and companies want to find the right fit for them. If you believe the company that offered you a job is not the perfect fit for your career aspirations, culture, or any other reason, it's best to reject the offer and continue your search if you can quell your anxiety and survive financially. Being as authentic and professional as possible through proactive communication will be critical to your success, and help you feel good not only about the job you take but also about the companies you leave behind.

Marlo Lyons is a certified career, executive, and team coach; an HR executive; and the award-winning author of *Wanted—A New Career: The Definitive Playbook for Transitioning to a New Career or Finding Your Dream Job.*

Transitioning into Your New Role

CHAPTER 19

Quitting Without Burning Bridges

by Rebecca Knight

Leaving your job can come with a range of emotions. If you've grown tired of your role or the company, you may be feeling more than ready to move on. (Who hasn't fantasized about walking into the boss's office, saying, "I quit!," and then marching straight out the door?) For many people, though, leaving a job is bittersweet. You're excited for the next opportunity, but you might miss friends, coworkers, and a role that you've enjoyed (and maybe you'll even miss your boss). But no matter why you're quitting, it's important to leave a good last

---

Adapted from "How to Quit Your Job Without Burning Bridges," on hbr.org, December 4, 2014 (product #H01QS6).

impression, since how you quit will stick in people's minds long after you're gone.

What the Experts Say

Chances are, you'll get a lot of practice quitting jobs over the course of your career. The average worker today stays at a job for 4.6 years, according to data from the Bureau of Labor Statistics. "People are more accustomed to the comings and goings of colleagues than in the past," says Daniel Gulati, the coauthor of *Passion and Purpose*. "It's all part and parcel of company life." And yet, there will inevitably be some curiosity about your departure. "Colleagues may be trying to read you and understand why you're leaving," he says. Remember, he says, "you set the tone." According to Len Schlesinger, a professor at Harvard Business School and the coauthor of *Just Start*, "The bookends—how you start and how you end—are the most important parts of any professional relationship." The trouble is that people tend to spend a lot of time preparing for and strategizing about their first impressions and rarely give much thought to their last ones. Quitting your job for any reason—whether it's because you're deeply unhappy or you're embarking on a new opportunity—"requires sensitivity and planning," says Schlesinger. Here's how to handle it.

Be flexible

To leave an organization with anything less than two weeks' notice is simply "bad form," warns Schlesinger. And while two weeks is customary, you might consider "offering to work even longer if you haven't already committed to a start date at another organization," he says. The higher up you are in an organization, the longer it will take to extricate yourself and possibly train the next person coming in, so you may need to give closer to a month if possible. On the other hand, giving too much notice—more than three months, say—is not necessarily wise, says Gulati. "The moment you tell people you're leaving, you're perceived as an outsider," he says. You most likely won't be invited to certain meetings, and team-bonding events will take on a different dynamic. "You don't want to be hanging around too long."

Tell your boss first

Once you've decided to resign, the first person you should tell is your manager. The reason is obvious: You "don't want your boss to hear the news from anyone else," says Schlesinger. After you've revealed your plans, though, "you're no longer in the driver's seat." Decisions surrounding the nature and timing of your departure are best left up to your supervisor. You may, however, weigh in on how your resignation is communicated, explains Gulati. Will the news be announced in a team meeting? In an email? Are you responsible for telling key people in the organization? "You want to establish that up front" to keep the rumor mill at bay, Gulati says.

Be transparent

While you're under no legal or moral obligation to reveal your next career move, it's worthwhile to take the "long view" on this one, advises Gulati. "In this hyperconnected world, your [former coworkers] are going to know all about your new role and new company" the minute you update your LinkedIn profile. When you're honest and straightforward about your plans, you "own the narrative," he says. "The more transparent you are, the more likely you are to preserve and build on the relationships you already have." Former coworkers are a crucial part of your network, and you want to keep those relationships intact.

Don't gossip

"There are no secrets and no off-the-record conversations in the workplace," says Schlesinger. If you give different reasons for your departure to different groups—if your boss hears one story, for example, while your close colleagues hear another—expect that you'll be Topic A at the watercooler. "Learn the essential lesson of being a politician: There is only one story, told one way, and you stick to it," he says. "That way nobody can ever say they heard anything different."

Be strategic about your time

Regardless of your reasons for quitting, you have one final responsibility to your company—and that is to engender an "orderly and positive transition," according to Schlesinger. "Your only orientation [during your notice period] is to make sure you don't leave your boss in a pickle," he adds. To that end, you need to "collaborate with your boss." Ask your manager for direction and close supervision on how you ought to tie up loose ends. After you leave, "you want your former boss and colleagues to feel nothing but positive about your professionalism," Schlesinger says.

Express gratitude

Even if you're ecstatic to be leaving your job, you need to adopt an appreciative mindset about the position and people you're leaving behind, says Gulati. As he points out, "Even in the worst situations, there are parts that you enjoy and colleagues you like working with. You need to be grateful for the things that went well." Modest farewell gifts or thoughtful notes to your direct supervisor, mentors, and other people you worked with leave a good impression. If, however, you're dealing with a supervisor or direct reports who are taking your departure personally by "acting emotionally or accusing you of disloyalty, you need to just chalk it up to collateral damage," says Gulati. "It's not productive to waste your time and energy trying to change their minds."

Beware the exit interview

It might be tempting to be brutally honest during your exit interview and offer up detailed information on everything that's wrong with your company. But Schlesinger warns against this overly negative approach. "The exit interview is not the time to give the feedback you wished you had given while you were a full-time employee," he says. His reasons are twofold. "First, you're not guaranteed anonymity; it's a small world. Second, your feedback is not going to change the organization." If you like your job and had a wonderful relationship with your boss but got a better offer, "feel free to talk about it, but don't feel obliged," he says. Gulati's exit interview advice: "No venting. And no emotional conversations."

Case study: Take the initiative to create a smooth transition

Nancy Twine had spent close to seven years at Goldman Sachs. She began her career in the commodities sales division and was later promoted to vice president. But Nancy felt she was at a crossroads. For the past two years, she had spent nights and weekends pursuing a side project: a business selling natural shampoos and soaps inspired by a family tradition of making those products from scratch. "I finally made a decision: I was going to leave my job and focus on my business full-time," she says, adding that it was important to her that she leave Goldman on good terms. "I had learned so much over the years, and I had built a lot of strong relationships."

She planned to give a month's notice because she knew from experience that abrupt departures cause turmoil on a team. When the moment came, she was honest with her boss. "I said I was going to pursue an entrepreneurial venture in the beauty business—that it was something I'd been wanting to do for a while and that now was the right time." Her manager took the news well, but she did ask whether Nancy would be willing to extend her notice period by two weeks. Nancy agreed on the spot. "I knew I could spare the time, and it would help smooth the transition."

During her remaining six weeks at the bank, Nancy put together a detailed spreadsheet of all her accounts and went over this information in several meetings with her boss. "I wanted to be a team member until the very end," she says.

Today Nancy is the CEO of Briogeo Hair Care. She is also the youngest African American woman to ever launch a line with Sephora, the cosmetics chain. "Even though what I do now is very different from my old job in finance," she says, "I use a lot of what I learned there in my day-to-day—how to be strategic, how to see a project through from start to finish, and how to communicate. It was the right decision to leave, but I am grateful to have worked there."

———————

Rebecca Knight is a future-of-work journalist based in Boston. Her work has been published in the *New York Times,* the BBC, *USA Today,* the *Boston Globe,* Business Insider, and the *Financial Times.* In 2023 she was a finalist for the Reuters Institute Fellowship at Oxford University.

CHAPTER 20

What to Say in an Exit Interview

by Rebecca Zucker

Given that most people will hold multiple jobs over the course of their professional lives, you may have the opportunity to participate in an exit interview at one or more points during your career. Not all organizations conduct exit interviews, but if you do have the opportunity to do one, it is a chance to provide a helpful point of view to the organization so that leadership can learn and continuously improve for current and future employees. Although the previous chapter warned about oversharing during your exit interview, depending on your situation, being professional in giving your employer some

---

Adapted from content posted on hbr.org, January 24, 2020 (product #H05DI0).

constructive feedback could benefit both you and the people you leave behind.

Whether you are leaving to pursue a new opportunity, escape a toxic leader or environment, seek better work-life balance, make a career change, or all of the above, you don't want to make the exit interview an emotional venting session. Be calm and constructive, sticking to the facts while being both open and direct in your responses. You'll want to include the following information in your feedback.

Your reason for leaving

This information is fairly straightforward. Perhaps you were approached, unsolicited, by an executive recruiter with an exciting new role that was also a step up in title and pay. Or maybe you are relocating to be closer to family or to support your partner's new job. Or perhaps you are burned out and need a break to reflect on what you really want in your career and life. Your reasons are helpful for the organization to know and can allow the exit interviewer to probe further in the appropriate areas.

How well your job was structured and if you had the appropriate tools to succeed

To what extent was your job meaningful and motivating, allowing you to do the work you most enjoy? Did your manager create opportunities for you to use your strengths? You'll also want to share the extent to which your manager supported you and helped you clear obstacles and whether you had the appropriate resources to do your job well. These include things like budget, people, and tools, such as the appropriate software to make your job easier.

Whether you had opportunities to learn and grow

According to a Gallup study, 32% of people leave their jobs because of a lack of career advancement or promotion opportunities. You'll want to share the extent to which you could see a viable career path in the organization and if you were given opportunities to gain new skills and experiences during your tenure. These opportunities could include stretch assignments and high-stakes projects that enabled you to grow in your career. You should also share whether your manager regularly provided actionable feedback (both positive and improvement feedback) that allowed you to learn continuously and get better at your job.

How you feel about your manager and other leaders

The exit interview is an opportunity to recognize good managers and other leaders, highlighting what made them so good, and to identify less-great ones. If your manager empowered you to make decisions and showed good emotional intelligence, that's helpful information for the organization. Just as helpful is knowing about those who may be detracting from a positive working environment or who are even a contributing factor to your decision to leave. Such a person may be a boss who demonstrates bullying behavior or manages by instilling fear. In particular, when multiple exit interviews echo the same negative feedback, the organization has even more incentive to act on it. Leadership might provide the manager in question with coaching to help increase their awareness and mitigate unproductive behaviors or, in more extreme cases, launch an investigation that may lead to further action. Rather than thinking of sharing this information as tattling on anyone, consider it as shining a light on a problem to be solved to make things better for your soon-to-be-former colleagues and the organization's future employees.

What you liked most about your job and the company

Include positive elements of your experience at the organization—what you liked and appreciated most about the job, your team, and the organization. Just as people need to hear positive feedback to know what they should continue doing, so do organizations. This information could include specific benefits offered, investments made in your learning and development, or an aspect of the company culture that you most valued.

Your top recommendations for improvement

Identify the top one or two areas that could benefit from improvement in the organization. These may also be the factors that would have kept you from leaving (if there are any). Your recommendations may include things like more flexible work options, more competitive compensation (data is always useful here if you are able to share this), a culture that is more welcoming of dissenting views, and better upward feedback mechanisms.

Taking the time to share the preceding information can help focus the organization's improvement efforts. Good leaders make things better for others, and the exit interview is a small but important way to contribute to this aim.

Rebecca Zucker is an executive coach and a founding partner at Next Step Partners, a leadership development firm. Her clients have included Amazon, Clorox, Morrison Foerster, Norwest Venture Partners, the James Irvine Foundation, and high-growth technology companies like DocuSign and Dropbox. You can follow her on X/Twitter @rszucker.

CHAPTER 21

Five Questions to Ask When Starting a New Role

by Michael D. Watkins

The actions you take during your first few months in a new job have a major impact on your success or failure. Build positive momentum early on, and it will propel you through your tenure. Make some early missteps, and you could face an uphill battle for the rest of your time in the job.

The biggest challenge leaders face during these periods is *staying focused on the right things*. You are

---

Adapted from "5 Questions to Ask When Starting a New Job," on hbr.org, April 9, 2019 (product #H04W39).

drinking from the proverbial fire hose while trying to get settled and figure out how to start having an impact. It's easy to take on too much or to waste your precious time. So, it helps to have a set of questions to guide you. Here are the five most important ones to ask—and to keep asking on a regular basis.

How Will I Create Value?

This is the single most important question. Why were you put in this role? What do key stakeholders expect you to accomplish? In what time frame? How will your progress be assessed? As you seek to answer this question, keep in mind that the real answer may not be what you were told when you were appointed or recruited for the job; it may also evolve as things progress and you learn more. Remember, too, that you will probably have multiple stakeholders, not just your boss, to satisfy and that they may have divergent views of what constitutes success. It's essential to understand the full set of expectations so that you can reconcile and satisfy them to the greatest degree possible.

How Am I Expected to Behave?

Unless you have been hired to change the culture of your new organization, you should strive to understand its most important norms of behavior. Think of culture as the organization's immune system. It exists primarily to prevent "wrong thinking" and "wrong behaving" from infecting the social organism. So there are risks in violating key norms of behavior; being viewed as someone who "doesn't belong here" can lead to isolation and, ultimately, to derailment. As you seek to understand the norms, keep in mind that they may differ across the organization. They may also vary according to the level at which you are operating: Success after promotion may be helped, in no small measure, by you showing up in different ways.

Whose Support Is Critical?

Because your success is likely to be affected by people over whom you have no direct authority, you need to build alliances. The starting point for doing this is to understand the political landscape of your new organization and learn to navigate it. Who has power and influence? Whose support is crucial, and why? Armed with insight into the *who*, you can focus on how you will secure their backing. This step usually involves more than just building relationships. You need to understand what others are trying to accomplish and how you can help them. Reciprocity is the firmest foundation on which to build allies.

How Will I Get Some Early Wins?

Leaders in transition energize people by getting early wins—quick, tangible improvements that create a sense of momentum in the organization. Done well, they build your credibility, accelerate your learning, and win you the right to make deeper changes. So, you need to identify the most promising ways to make a quick, positive impact and then organize to do so as efficiently and effectively as possible.

What Skills Do I Need to Develop to Excel in This Role?

As Marshall Goldsmith, a renowned executive coach, put it, "What got you here won't get you there." The skills and abilities that got you to this point in your career may not be the ones (or the only ones) you need to be successful in your new job, and it's all too easy to fall into the comfort-zone trap. Put another way, to become fully effective in your new role, you will probably have to do some personal development. This doesn't mean you can't get off to a good start immediately, but the sooner you understand what new capabilities you need to excel in the role, the better. Failure to grasp this essential point diminishes the potential for future career advancement.

Ask yourself these five questions as you start a new role, and keep asking them regularly. Set aside 30 minutes at the end of each week to reflect on whether the answers are still clear or have changed in any way. Doing so will enable you to stay on the right track through your transition and beyond.

———————

Michael D. Watkins is a cofounder of Genesis Advisers, a professor at IMD Business School, and the author of *The First 90 Days* and *Master Your Next Move* (both Harvard Business Review Press, 2013 and 2019, respectively).

CHAPTER 22

Starting a New Job Remotely

by Art Markman

You should always be proactive about getting acclimated to a new role. But when you're starting a job remotely—and won't work side by side with your new colleagues much or at all—it's especially imperative that you take initiative in getting up to speed. Here are five things you can do to fill the gaps and minimize the bumps as you make the transition into the new job.

Schedule a Lot of Brief Check-ins with Colleagues

One of the hardest things about starting with a new company is that each organization has a culture of its

Adapted from "Starting a New Job—Remotely," on hbr.org, May 4, 2020 (product #H05LLQ).

own. That culture is often made up of unspoken goals and norms and is often wrapped up in a unique language that members of your new team have already learned to speak. In my consulting work, I've often been baffled by terms that employees regularly use inside companies but that have no meaning outside it.

You learn these subtle aspects of the workplace through everyday interactions with colleagues, hearing conversations and having discussions about what other people are working on. You pick up on workplace jargon and surmise from these conversations what activities are valued and what styles of work are appreciated.

Under normal circumstances, these interactions are a natural part of being in the office. Now, you're going to have to manufacture them. Reach out to your new colleagues, and set up 10- to 15-minute one-on-one discussions. These can be by phone or video and shouldn't be one-offs. Try to meet with your colleagues regularly to mimic the short, informal interactions you'd have in person. Use these conversations to ask questions you may have about your current projects, but make sure to ask people what they are working on too so that they have a chance to describe their work. Pay attention to any implicit statements about what they think is most important.

Rapidly Assemble Your Mentoring Team

Throughout your career, you need a team of people who will mentor you. There are two types of mentors who are particularly important inside your current company.

The first is someone who knows how things get done in the firm and can help you navigate the procedures for everything from getting reimbursed for expenses to accessing equipment. The second is a person who is well connected throughout the organization and can introduce you to people you need to know.

Ordinarily, you can afford to develop these relationships slowly. When you start working for a company remotely, though, you want to identify initial candidates to play these roles for you as soon as possible. You can't just make your way around the office, finding colleagues who might point you in the right direction. Instead, your requests are likely to involve emails or queries on Slack, and those responses can be slow. If you put some good mentors in place quickly, you make it easier to be productive quickly.

However, don't feel as if you have to commit to having these people as mentors throughout your tenure at the company. The downside to choosing fast is that you may settle on someone who is available but isn't the perfect fit. As you get to know the organization better, you may choose to reach out to other people to be your guides. But having someone early on is better than having nobody.

Announce Yourself as New

When you start a job in an office, people tend to notice they're seeing a new face around. And under normal circumstances, you can expect people to introduce themselves and even offer help.

That is not going to happen when you're the new person in the virtual office. Ideally, your new manager will introduce you, but you'll most likely "meet" many of your new colleagues as one of a sea of faces in a virtual meeting. That means you need to be more explicit about announcing yourself as the new person in the office. If there is a team meeting, see if you can get a moment to introduce yourself. Also, let people know you're the new person in forums like Slack and by sending some brief emails to other people in your unit. These steps may be hard if you don't like to call attention to yourself. But you want to let folks know that you're new and that you would appreciate their help in getting settled. Many of your colleagues would like to welcome you; they just need more explicit reminders to do so than they might otherwise.

Ask for Help

In the office, colleagues often pick up on a quizzical facial expression or tone of voice and may offer assistance if they think you need it. On video and phone meetings, it will be hard for people to see if you are confused or aren't keeping up. As a rule, when there is something you need, say so.

You might be worried that your colleagues won't want to help. After all, everyone has a lot going on. Yet research by Vanessa Bohns and Francis Flynn suggests that people are often much more willing to help than you believe they will be.[1] So, don't wait for offers of assistance. Ask for what you need.

Keep a Daily Diary

When you're in the office, it's easy to take care of problems as they arise. You can often just get up from your desk and find someone to help you solve them. When you're working at home, if you dash off an email or a note on Slack asking for an answer, your request may get lost in the noise. And if it's a small issue, you may even forget to follow up.

So end each day by going back through your schedule and making some notes about how things went. Write down the tasks you accomplished and the obstacles you faced. If there are particular issues that are still unresolved, highlight them. Then, when you have your next meeting with a supervisor or a colleague, raise those issues and ask for their perspective.

Your memory for what happens each day is strongest around things that are familiar, normal parts of work. That means that you are the least likely to remember the novel aspects of your new workplace—which are precisely the elements that you need the most help with. Writing down the events of your day while they are still fresh in your mind is a great way to overcome this bias.

It's never easy being the new person on a team. But by being proactive, you can more smoothly acclimate to the organization and prove your value quickly.

Art Markman is the Annabel Irion Worsham Centennial Professor of Psychology, Human Dimensions of Organizations, and Marketing and the vice provost for academic affairs at the University of Texas at Austin. He has written more than 150 scholarly papers on various topics, including reasoning, decision-making, and motivation. His most recent book is *Bring Your Brain to Work* (Harvard Business Review Press, 2019).

NOTE

1. Vanessa K. Bohns and Francis J. Flynn, "'Why Didn't You Just Ask?' Underestimating the Discomfort of Help-Seeking," *Journal of Experimental Social Psychology* 46, no. 2 (March 2010): 402–409, https://doi.org/10.1016/j.jesp.2009.12.015.

Index

Index

Smart advice and inspiration from a source you trust.

If you enjoyed this book and want more comprehensive guidance on essential professional skills, turn to the HBR Guides Boxed Set. Packed with the practical advice you need to succeed, this seven-volume collection provides smart answers to your most pressing work challenges, from writing more effective emails and delivering persuasive presentations to setting priorities and managing up and across.

Harvard Business Review Guides

Available in paperback or ebook format. Plus, find downloadable tools and templates to help you get started.

- Better Business Writing
- Building Your Business Case
- Buying a Small Business
- Coaching Employees
- Delivering Effective Feedback
- Finance Basics for Managers
- Getting the Mentoring You Need
- Getting the Right Work Done

- Leading Teams
- Making Every Meeting Matter
- Managing Stress at Work
- Managing Up and Across
- Negotiating
- Office Politics
- Persuasive Presentations
- Project Management

HBR.ORG/GUIDES

Buy for your team, clients, or event.
Visit hbr.org/bulksales for quantity discount rates.

Notes

Notes

Notes

Notes

Notes